PR
6019
.09
Z52585
1985

A

DISCARD
DISCARD

James Joyce

LITERATURE AND LIFE SERIES

[Formerly Modern Literature and World Dramatists]

Selected list of titles:

Complete list of titles in the series available from publisher on request.

James Joyce

Bernard Benstock

Frederick Ungar Publishing Co.
New York

Grateful Acknowledgment is made to Random House, Inc., for permission to quote from *Ulysses* by James Joyce, Copyright 1914, 1918 by Margaret Caroline Anderson. Copyright renewed, 1942, 1946 by Nora Joseph Joyce. Copyright 1934, by Modern Library, Inc. Copyright renewed, 1961, by Lucia and George Joyce.

From *Finnegans Wake* by James Joyce. Copyright 1939 by James Joyce. Copyright renewed © 1967 by George Joyce and Lucia Joyce. Reprinted by permission of Viking Penguin Inc., and The Society of Authors as literary representative of the James Joyce Estate.

From *Dubliners* by James Joyce. Copyright 1916 by B.W. Huebsch. Definitive text Copyright © 1967 by the Estate of James Joyce. Reprinted by permission of Viking Penguin Inc., and Jonathan Cape Ltd. as executors of the James Joyce Estate.

From *A Portrait of the Artist as a Young Man* by James Joyce. Copyright 1916 by B.W. Huebsch. Copyright renewed 1944 by Nora Joyce. Definitive text copyright © 1964 by the Estate of James Joyce. Reprinted by permission of Viking Penguin Inc., and Jonathan Cape Ltd. as executors of the James Joyce Estate.

From *Collected Poems* by James Joyce. Copyright 1918 by James Joyce. Copyright 1927, 1936 by James Joyce. Copyright renewed 1946 by Nora Joyce. Reprinted by permission of Viking Penguin Inc., and Jonathan Cape Ltd. as executors of the James Joyce Estate.

From *Exiles* by James Joyce. Copyright 1918 by B.W. Huebsch. Copyright renewed 1945 by Nora Joyce. Copyright 1951 by The Viking Press Inc. Copyright renewed © 1979 by Viking Penguin Inc. Reprinted by permission of Viking Penguin Inc., and Jonathan Cape Ltd. as executors of the James Joyce Estate.

Library of Congress Cataloging in Publication Data

Benstock, Bernard.
    James Joyce.

        (Literature and life series)
        Bibliography: p.
        Includes index.
        1. Joyce, James, 1882-1941—Criticism and interpretation.
        I. Title. II. Series
PR6019.09Z52583   1985   823.912   84-28048
ISBN 0-8044-2047-5
ISBN 0-8044-6037-X (pbk.)

This Book is Dedicated to

Tom Staley

author,

bibliophile,

chauffeur,

detective,

editor,

friend,

gourmet,

host,

iconoclast,

Joycean,

kingpin,

lecturer,

mixologist,

neighbor,

oenophile,

provost, etc.

Contents

Chronology

1882   2 February. Born at 41 Brighton Square West, Rathgar, middle-class suburb of Dublin, Ireland. Parents: John Stanislaus Joyce, formerly of Cork City, tax collector and political employee; Mary Jane Joyce, nee Murray.

1884   Brother Stanislaus born. Remained closest sibling during their early adult lives.

1888   Joyce family moved to Bray, as the family was enlarging. The house on Martello Terrace is the scene in the opening chapter of *A Portrait of the Artist as a Young Man*, the Vances actually having lived on the same street. In September James Joyce is enrolled at Clongowes Wood College, near Sallins in County Kildare, at the rather early age of "half-past six."

1891   6 October. Death of Charles Stewart Parnell (remembered eleven years later in "Ivy Day in the Committee Room"). John Joyce remains a staunch Parnellite (the Christmas dinner scene in *A Portrait*) and loses political patronage, the beginning of the family financial troubles and the withdrawal of James Joyce from Clongowes.

1892   Move to Blackrock (chapter 2 of *A Portrait*), still respectable suburban.

1893   Move to northeast quadrant of Dublin as the family finances decline, and a series of many such moves remain in the offing. James Joyce enrolled as a day student at Belvedere College, also a Jesuit school.

1894   Visit with his father to Cork in February to sell off the remaining family properties. James Joyce as prize-winning scholarship student. (Both events portrayed in the second chapter of *A Portrait*.)

1898   Completion of studies at Belvedere and enrollment in University College (last chapter of *A Portrait*).

1900   James Joyce reads his paper on "Drama and Life" at the Literary and Historical Society (dramatized in the extant segment of *Stephen Hero*), and has his article on Ibsen published in the prestigious *Fortnightly Review*. His writing career while a university student well under way, including a play that he later destroyed, which apparently bore the title of *A Brilliant Career*.

1901   An essay, "The Day of the Rabblement," attacking the "Irish Literary Theatre" and its narrow nationalism, was refused for *St. Stephen's* by Jesuit advisor, and consequently published as part of a pamphlet by Joyce himself. (Available in *The Collected Writing of James Joyce*.)

1902   Graduation from University College, Dublin, and departure for Paris (closing pages of *A Portrait*), presumably in order to study medicine. Begins reviewing books for the *Daily Express* (as does Gabriel Conroy in "The Dead" and Stephen Dedalus in *Ulysses*). Returns temporarily to Dublin for Christmas with the family.

1903   Time spent in Paris mostly reading at the Bibliothèque Ste. Geneviève, rather than attending lectures on medicine. Returns in April to Dublin because of his mother's illness; she dies 13 August with her son at her bedside.

1904   Joyce at work on various writing projects: an essay, "A
        Portrait of the Artist," from which his first novel
        evolved; poems published in journals that would later
        be included in *Chamber Music;* stories in *The Irish
        Homestead* that would be included in *Dubliners.* Joyce
        leaves his father's deteriorating home, and in March is
        employed as a teacher at the Clifton School in Dalkey
        (chapter 2 of *Ulysses*). Various temporary residences,
        including in September the Martello Tower in
        Sandycove rented by Oliver St. John Gogarty (chapter
        1 of *Ulysses*). On 10 June he meets Nora Barnacle, in
        Dublin from Galway and working at Finn's Hotel; on 8
        October he and Nora leave Ireland for the Continent,
        where the promise of a job teaching English at a
        Berlitz School fades in Zurich but eventually
        materializes in Pola on the Istrian peninsula.

1905   Move to Trieste to teach at the Berlitz School there,
        where on 27 July son Giorgio is born. *Chamber Music*
        and first version of *Dubliners* submitted to a Dublin
        publisher. Stanislaus joins them in Trieste, where he
        lives until his death in 1955.

1906   Temporary move to Rome for a job at a bank. Two
        more stories added to *Dubliners.*

1907   Dissatisfied with Rome the Joyces return to Trieste,
        where James Joyce gives private English lessons.
        Daughter Lucia born on 26 July. *Chamber Music*
        published by Elkin Matthews. After a bout with
        rheumatic fever Joyce writes "The Dead," and in
        September scraps the 26 chapters of *Stephen Hero* to
        reconstitute his material into *A Portrait of the Artist
        as a Young Man.* Joyce writes articles for the Trieste
        newspaper *Il Piccolo della Sera* (included in *Critical
        Writings*).

1908   First three chapters of *A Portrait* completed, but the
       manuscript lies follow thereafter for several years.

1909   Two return trips to Dublin: first to sign a contract with
       Maunsel and Co. for publication of *Dubliners;* then to
       represent a Triestine consortium to set up the first
       motion picture theater in Dublin. Malicious gossip in
       Dublin about Nora results in the letters to her that
       were eventually published long after their deaths, as
       well as the subject matter for the play *Exiles.* Joyce's
       sister Eva comes back with her brother to Trieste to
       live with them.

1910   Joyce returns to Trieste and in his wake the cinema
       theater folds and new plans for publishing *Dubliners*
       also in jeopardy.

1911   An unproductive year comprised of house-moving,
       failure of *Dubliners* publication, family quarrels, poverty,
       drunkenness, dissatisfaction with Trieste.

1912   A July visit to Dublin and Galway of the Joyce family,
       which will prove to be his last stay on Irish soil.
       Enraged printer burns manuscript of *Dubliners* and
       any possible publication looks more remote than ever.
       Joyce leaves Ireland, leveling his blast in a broadside,
       "Gas from a Burner" (in *Collected Writings*).

1913   First contact with Ezra Pound, through W.B. Yeats.

1914   *Dubliners* finally published in Dublin by Grant Richards,
       the original contractor for the book. *A Portrait of the
       Artist as a Young Man* serialized in London in the
       Egoist, spurring Joyce into finishing the last two
       chapters. *Ulysses* begins to take shape. The turn in

Joyce's fortunes counterbalanced by the beginning of the Great War in August.

1915   As a British subject Joyce faced interment by the Austrian authorities in Trieste, but after pledging to remain neutral he and his family are allowed to go into exile in Zurich. Stanislaus interred. *Exiles* completed before the move to Switzerland, and *Ulysses* well under way. British Royal Literary Fund grant.

1916   *A Portrait of the Artist as a Young Man* published in New York. Joyce awarded a grant from the British Treasury Fund.

1917   First three chapters of *Ulysses* written. Financial support for Joyce from Harriet Weaver. Joyce's first of many subsequent eye operations.

1918   *Exiles* published in London, and first chapters of *Ulysses* begin being serialized in the *Little Review* in the United States. Joyce becomes involved with the English Players in Zurich and receives further financial support from Mrs. Harold McCormick.

1919   Mrs. McCormick's allowance ends when Joyce refuses to be psychoanalyzed by Carl Jung. The *Egoist* also serializing *Ulysses*. The end of the war and the Joyces return to now-Italian Trieste.

1920   Joyce finds Trieste changed and accepts Ezra Pound's suggestion that he move to Paris, where the Joyces take up residence in July. *Ulysses* serialization ends when the *Little Review* loses a court case brought against Joyce's book by the Society for the Prevention of Vice.

1921   *Ulysses* completed and undergoing constant revision
        as Joyce searches for a publisher courageous enough to
        risk publishing it.

1922   Under the imprint of her Shakespeare and Company
        Paris bookshop Sylvia Beach publishes *Ulysses*, an
        advance copy placed in Joyce's hands on his 40th
        birthday. Against her husband's wishes Nora takes the
        children for a visit to her native Galway during the
        Irish Civil War, and her train is fired on.

1923   Joyce begins to write the first bits and pieces of what he
        called during the next sixteen years, *Work in Progress*
        (eventually titled *Finnegans Wake*).

1924   Herbert Gorman's biography of Joyce and commission-
        ed by him is published in New York. First fragment of
        Work in Progress published in *The Transatlantic
        Review*. (The pattern of Joyce's life takes shape:
        sporadic work on *Finnegans Wake*, constant changes
        of residence in Paris, an active social life amid the
        newly established affluence, yearly vacations through-
        out Europe, and the series of eye operations that left
        Joyce partially blind.)

1927   Publication of the second book of poems, *Pomes
        Penyeach*, by Shakespeare and Company. The first of
        many installments of *Work in Progress* in Eugene
        Jolas's *transition*.

1929   French translation of *Ulysses*, at which Joyce assisted,
        appears, as does *Our Exagmination Round His
        Factification for Incamination of Work in Progress*,
        twelve pioneer essays on the as-yet incomplete
        Finnegans Wake by such writers as Samuel Beckett,
        William Carlos Williams, et al.

1930   Publication of the first book-length study of *Ulysses*, Stuart Gilbert's *James Joyce's Ulysses.*

1931   Nora Barnacle and James Joyce officially married at a registry office in London, so that Giorgio and Lucia could legally inherit. Death of John Stanislaus Joyce on 29 December.

1932   Birth on 15 February of the Joyces' first grandchild, Stephen James Joyce, to Giorgio and Helen Joyce. Joyce writes "Ecce Puer," celebrating the birth and mourning the death of his father. Lucia suffers the first of many subsequent mental breakdowns which will eventually lead to permanent hospitalization.

1933   *Ulysses* wins court verdict as not pornographic, paving the way for publication in the United States. Lucia temporarily hospitalized near Zurich.

1934   *Ulysses* published in New York by Random House. Frank Budgen's *James Joyce and the Making of Ulysses* published.

1936   *Collected Poems* published in New York.

1936   The last fragment of *Work in Progress* prior to the completion of *Finnegans Wake* published in London.

1938   Progress completed on the new Joyce work and publication arranged in New York and London.

1939   4 May. Publication of *Finnegans Wake,* an advance copy reaching Joyce in time for his 57th birthday. War declared in September, and the Joyces immediately leave Paris for St. Gérand-le-Puy near Vichy, close to where Lucia is hospitalized.

1940   Herbert Gorman's *James Joyce,* a revised and updated
        version, published. France falls to the Nazis, and by
        year's end the Joyces manage to secure permission to
        enter neutral Switzerland and take up exile again in
        Zurich.

1941   13 January. Death of James Joyce in Zurich after
        surgery on a perforated ulcer. Burial in a pauper's
        grave in Fluntern cemetery in Zurich, without the last
        rites of the Church. Death of Nora Barnacle Joyce in
        1951, and separate burial in Fluntern. The two bodies
        were reburied together in 1966.

Legend

Reference throughout to the texts by James Joyce are to the current American editions, and page numbers are prefaced as follows:

AP   *A Portrait of the Artist as a Young Man* (Penguin).

D   *Dubliners* (Penguin).

E   *Exiles* (Penguin).

U   *Ulysses* (Vintage).

FW   *Finnegans Wake* (Penguin). Page numbers followed by inclusive line numbers.

SH   *Stephen Hero* (New Directions)

James Joyce

1

In the Beginning

The World He Found, the Life He Led

Candlemas has been celebrated in the Roman Catholic Church at least since the seventh century. The blessing of the candles and the penitential procession commemorate the presentation of Jesus in the temple of Jerusalem and also the purification of Mary forty days after the birth of Jesus, and the feast has historically developed from the Christological to the Marian over the centuries. For James Joyce his birthday on the second of February, the day of the celebration of Candlemas, was of personal importance, as various friends, especially during the Paris years in the nineteen-twenties and thirties, testify in their remembrances of the festivities with which he observed his birthday. His reliance on the momentousness of the occasion caused him to attempt to arrange the publications of *Ulysses* and *Finnegans Wake* to coincide with the birthdays of 1922 and 1939, even if only a single advance copy could be put into his hands on that important day. (Both *Ulysses* and *Finnegans Wake,* concluding as they do with the soliloquies of Molly Bloom and Anna Livia Plurabelle, can be shown to progress from the Christological to the Marian.) Frank Budgen, Joyce's close acquaintance in the Zurich days during World War One, recalls that on his thirty-fifth birthday, celebrated by Joyce as the middle of the road of his life, Joyce borrowed Budgen's flat for an illicit liaison of sorts with a

1

woman who reminded him of Molly Bloom, for which he
provided a Hebrew candelabra as fitting for Candlemas Day.
Both as a desecration and as a consecration, this act typifies
James Joyce's approach to the symbolic import he attached to
everything from incidents in his own life to aspects of his
literary creations.

The year of Joyce's birth, 1882, may also have had some
mystic significance for him, but in many ways it was a quite
ordinary one historically. The Ireland of his birth certainly had
its moments of turmoil that year, but the British Empire of
which it was still a constituent element was relatively tranquil
despite the Land League agitation in Ireland, and the Easter
Rising that would precipitate the rupture between Ireland and
Britain still several decades away. Among those also born in
1882 was Eamon de Valera, a mathematician turned politician
by the Irish troubles, who eventually became head of state in a
new Ireland born out of the violence of the Rising and the
ensuing "Troubles." Had De Valera been born in Ireland he
would have been executed in 1916 along with the other leaders
of the abortive Rising, but his American passport saved his
life, and he went on to have a long life as Ireland's major
political figure. Another of Joyce's "immediate" contem-
poraries, born as was Joyce in Dublin, was the Irish writer of
whimsy, James Stephens, whom Joyce assumed—probably
quite arbitrarily, since Stephens kept his birth year mysteriously
secret—was born on the same day as himself and in the same
city. Stephen's actual birth year is still in dispute, and may well
have been 1880 rather than 1882, but Joyce was capable of
making legends—even for others. When Joyce found himself
facing possible blindness in Paris in the early thirties, and
Finnegans Wake still unfinished, he fastened onto Stephens,
also a resident in Paris, as the ideal writer to complete the
Wake, because of the coincidence of birth date and birthplace,
and the added coincidence of names. In actual fact it was Nikos
Kazantzakis, the Greek novelist, who was also born on 2
February 1882, but that coincidence would have been of no
value to James Joyce.

Across the Irish Sea in England the major woman novelist of the century was born barely a week before Joyce, and although throughout their lives the two writers never met, nor made any attempt to meet, their parallel courses as major exponents of modernist literature contain fascinating coincidences, corollaries, and contrasts. Not quite coincidental in their paralleled lives was the death of Virginia Woolf by suicide barely two months after the death on an operating table in Zurich of James Joyce on 13 January 1941. The Second World War had driven him once again into exile in neutral Switzerland, and driven her, along with a life of numerous anxieties, to her self-inflicted death.

Across the North Atlantic in Canada in 1882 Percy Wyndham Lewis was born, with whom Joyce shared a friendship with Ezra Pound, and by extension with T. S. Eliot as well, and Joyce walked at least part way down the road to modernism with him, although he eventually parted company when Wyndham Lewis inclined toward the way that led to Mussolini and Hitler. In addition, 1882 was the birth year of such diverse writers as Jean Giraudoux in France, Sigrid Undset in Sweden, and A. A. Milne in England, writers who would remain significantly remote from the basic characteristics of modernism, although an inclusion of Georges Braque and Igor Stravinsky among those born that year demonstrates just how seminal 1882 was for modernism in the other arts.

For the British Isles, and the Empire generally, it was a year of relative peace and tranquility. The Zulu Wars were several years in the past, fit subjects for the adventure literature of a generation or two of young boys. The Transvaal Revolt of 1880-81 (the so-called First Boer War) had been put down by the British, and the Second Boer War was still many years in the future. Although what has become known as the Age of Equipoise, the middle years of Queen Victoria's reign, was past history, a sense of stability within the Empire and throughout most of Europe continued at the time. And for Central Europe the balance of power sought to assure that stability was

hammered into place in 1882 by the signing of the Triple
Alliance: Italy now joined the Dual Alliance of Germany and
the Austro-Hungarian Empire. It would require more than
three decades for the various alliances and ententes (Russia
signing with the Triple Alliance in 1887; France with Russia,
Britain with France, Russia with Britain thereafter) to
rearrange themselves, disintegrate, and finally collapse into
the Great War of 1914.

Not that 1882 was without incident. On the eleventh of June
riots broke out in Egypt against foreign rule, and the British
consul general was among the wounded. The British retaliated
with a naval bombardment of Alexandria in which two
thousand were killed, and landed ground forces in support of
British subjects and the investment in the Suez Canal—their
French partners in the ownership of the Canal abstained as
governments changed in Paris. The victorious English troops
captured the rebel Egyptian leader and banished him, and for a
while the cry of the fellaheen, "Egypt for the Egyptians" (a cry
that must have had echoes in Irish ears) was stilled. The
victorious British general, a hero also of the Zulu War and the
Boer Wars, was the Dublin-born Sir Garnet Wolseley, whom
Molly Bloom in the closing pages of *Ulysses* recalls as the hero
of the Sudan campaign and the Second Boer War. (Wolseley
also figures in *Finnegans Wake* for his role in the Crimean
War, where an Irishman is reported to have "soldiered a bit
with Wolsey under the assumed name of Blanco Fusilovna
Bucklovitch" (*FW* 49.7-9).

The British Secretary for War at the time of the Egyptian
campaign was H. C. E. Childers, a name that any reader of
Finnegans Wake could not resist conjuring with, and the
Childers surname has echoes through later Irish and British
events. Hugh Culling Eardley Childers was a cabinet member
in all three of the Gladstone administrations and a staunch
supporter of Home Rule for Ireland, a stand that cost him his
Parliament seat in 1885. His cousin was the author Robert
Erskine Childers, an officer in the Boer War, who later landed
guns in Ireland for the Irish Volunteers, but also fought for

Britain in the First World War. He remained a committed Irish Nationalist nonetheless and a Sinn Fein politician, and was executed by the Irish Free State during the 1922 Civil War as an IRA gunman. (His son was quite recently President of the Republic of Ireland.) It is H. C. E. Childers who appears momentarily in *Finnegans Wake*, a father figure certainly ("Pity poor Haveth Childers Everywhere with Mudder!" [*FW* 535.34]), but also represented by his children: "their childer and their napirs and their napirs' childers napirs" (*FW* 598.35-36).

A more immediate and disruptive event in the year 1882 occurred much nearer to home, and consequently much nearer to Joyce, in Dublin's Phoenix Park. The newly appointed chief secretary for Ireland, Lord Frederick Cavendish, and the under-secretary, Thomas Burke, were assassinated in front of the Vice-Regal Lodge by members of the Irish National Invincibles. Lord Cavendish had just arrived that day, 6 May 1882, having replaced William "Buckshot" Forster, who had resigned as chief secretary when Gladstone allowed Charles Stewart Parnell to be released from Kilmainham Jail. The Phoenix Park Murders reverberate throughout *Finnegans Wake*, the park itself serving as the essential locus, as well as the Garden of Eden, a Crimean battlefield, and Waterloo. Nonetheless, in the comic patchwork of the *Wake* there are few specific indicators of that particularly gory incident (the weapons used were ten-inch surgical knives purchased in Bond Street and smuggled into Ireland), apparently too grim a detail for casual treatment, although few allusions to Phoenix Park are free from association with the murders. It is in *Ulysses*, however, that direct reference to the event has its unusual presence, and, primarily because Joyce himself was born only three months before the murders, the association becomes mysterious and even mystic in quality.

When Miles Crawford, the newspaper editor, discusses the murders in *Ulysses*, twenty-two years have elapsed, and the incident for him is little more than a journalistic coup: "That was the smartest piece of journalism ever known," he insists to

Stephen Dedalus. "That was in eightyone, sixth of May, time of the invincibles, murder in the Phoenix park, before you were born, I suppose" (*U* 136). Had the murders actually taken place in 1881, that would have been before Stephen was born, since Stephen is twenty-two in 1904, having the same birth year as James Joyce. The rather dotty editor is certainly capable of getting the date wrong, but it is surprising that Leopold Bloom quite independently makes the same mistake: "He vividly recollected when the occurrence alluded to took place as well as yesterday, some scores of years previously, in the days of the land troubles when it took the civilised world by storm, figuratively speaking, early in the eighties, eightyone to be correct, when he was just turned fifteen" (*U* 629). Some chroniclers of the fictional life of Leopold Bloom assume that Bloom's birthday is indeed the sixth of May, and it is odd that in a narrative construction in which so many exact dates are known, Bloom's birthday is not—although if the murders occurred on his actual birthday, he would surely be expected to remember it just that way.

The repeated inaccuracy of the dating of the Phoenix Park Murders suggests a purposeful dissociation of the bloody occurrence with the year of the author's own birth. Joyce's enthusiasm for his birthday and his distaste for violence may well have been responsible for the dissociation. In *Ulysses* he locates the Circe chapter in Bella Cohen's brothel, but changes the real address of 82 Tyrone Street to 81:

BLOOM

Is this Mrs Mack's?

ZOE

No, eightyone. Mrs Cohen's. (*U* 475)

Clive Hart also notes that in *Finnegans Wake* Joyce "emended '82 Mabbot's Mall' to '81 bis Mabbot's Mall' ... [and] may have been acting in accordance with some superstition regarding the date of his birth." Given Joyce's amalgam of personal superstition and meaningful coincidences, it is worth noting that Leopold Bloom spent the summer of 1882 attempting to square the circle, and at other times during that year he "had advocated during nocturnal perambulations the political theory of colonial (e.g. Canadian) expansion and the evolutionary theories of Charles Darwin, expounded in *The Descent of Man* and *The Origin of Species"* (*U* 716), perhaps inspired by the death in 1882 of Charles Darwin. Others who died in the year of Joyce's birth were Benjamin Disraeli, Anthony Trollope, and Dante Gabriel Rossetti (and in America, Henry Wadsworth Longfellow), following the death of Thomas Carlyle the previous year and that of George Eliot the year before. And Karl Marx was to die in London in 1883.

Ulysses also records the news of how Leopold Bloom inadvertently celebrated the sixth birthday of James Joyce and Stephen Dedalus: "in support of his political convictions, [he] had climbed up into a secure position amid the ramifications of a tree on Northumberland road to see the entrance (2 February 1888) into the capital of a demonstrative torchlight procession of 20,000, divided into 120 trade corporations, bearing 2,000 torches in escort of the marquess of Ripon and John Morley" (*U* 716-17). Bloom obviously supported these Liberal advocates of Home Rule, but six years earlier, when Joyce was born, Parnell was in jail in Dublin because of Land League agitation, and Gladstone as yet no supporter of Home Rule for Ireland.

Joyce's life took shape around the events of a tumultuous period of European history, framed by Irish Land League agitation at his birth and the darkest period of World War Two at his death. His Irish roots, his Jesuit education, the economic decline of his father's fortunes, the fierce independence of his spirit, and the intensity of his dedication to the integrity of the creative artist contribute to the complex personality irrecoverable by biography. Joyce, who casually claimed that he invented nothing, sank all of his own experiences—and those of people around him—into his art, so that readers aware of the autobiographical coincidences tended to assume direct correlations between Joyce's fictive selves and Joyce himself. On the other hand, even the finest biography of Joyce fails to capture the psychological, spiritual, and sexual personality, since it attempts to read the person through the personae of the fiction. His own life for Joyce had been the base metals from which he alchemically made gold, and fashioned that gold into artifacts that at first gave the illusion of realistic portraiture but later took on complex and exotic shapes. The Stephen Dedalus who matures from infancy to early adulthood in *A Portrait of the Artist as a Young Man* and is frozen in time at age twenty-two in *Ulysses* parallels in his life that of the young James Joyce, while the Shem the Penman of *Finnegans Wake* carries the parallel into futuristic caricature.

Joyce's father, John Stanislaus Joyce, carved out for himself a Dublin reputation as a drinker, storyteller, and pub tenor. From a propertied Cork family that boasted connections with Daniel O'Connell, the engineer of Catholic Emancipation in Ireland, John Joyce committed himself to the cause of Charles Stewart Parnell, and committed his son James to it as well. John Joyce's economic fortunes declined rapidly during the years of his son's adolescence, and his political ties to Parnell, whose fortunes as the political hope of Irish Home Rule declined with the divorce scandal in which he was involved, cost Joyce's father his political job. The slippage of the Dedalus family from genteel respectability in *A Portrait* to a hand-to-mouth existence mirrors fairly accurately that of John Joyce's household, and the topographical features in the novel graph the demise from suburban residences to the north Dublin tenements, as Stephen's educational life moves in parallel from that of a boarding pupil at Clongowes Wood College to that of a day student at Belvedere College, with an interval in which the family is being jolted onto a new course leading toward poverty and Stephen is between schools. In Joyce's life part of that interval was spent at a Christian Brothers school, but that ignominy is excised from the fictional history, where Stephen is exclusively educated by the Jesuits, the Christian Brothers sneeringly characterized by his father as fit only to handle the "Mickey Muds" and "Paddy Stinks." John Joyce's checkered career spanned eighty-one years, but in Joyce's fiction it is succinctly capsulized in Stephen Dedalus's memorable description of his father as "A medical student, an oarsman, a tenor, an amateur actor, a shouting politician, a small landlord, a small investor, a drinker, a good fellow, a storyteller, somebody's secretary, something in a distillery, a taxgatherer, a bankrupt and at present a praiser of his own past" (*AP* 241).

Joyce's mother, May Murray Joyce, suffered the decline of the family into poverty and her husband's drunkenness, shored by her Catholic faith and her expectations that her eldest son James would find his vocation in the priesthood. Her counterpart in *A Portrait* expresses her disappointment and resentment as she watches her son go off to his lectures at the National University: "—Ah, it's a scandalous shame for you, Stephen, said his mother, and you'll live to rue the day you set your foot in that place. I know how it has changed you" (*AP* 175). The May Goulding Dedalus of *Ulysses* is even more memorable as the ghost haunting her profligate son whom he attempts to exorcise from his guilt-ridden consciousness and his presumably liberated conscience. It was May Joyce's terminal cancer that brought her son back from his first attempt at self-exile in Paris when he was twenty-one, where Joyce first assumed he would study medicine. His father's telegram is reconstructed in *Ulysses* in its simple structure, "Mother dying come home father" (*U* 42).

Dublin in the year 1882 was no stranger to untimely death. Infant mortality in particular was extremely high, one of the highest per capita in the entire world, not a surprising situation considering the poverty level at which a majority of the population lived—80 percent in substandard slum tenements. The Joyce family fared comparatively well, as befitted their still-middle-class respectability during the first years of family raising, ten children surviving infancy between 1882 and 1893 (one dying in infancy the next year), although John Joyce later claimed that there were some sixteen or seventeen, himself displaying a tendency to make hyperbole out of reality. One of Joyce's younger siblings died during adolescence, an incident that he transformed for inclusion in his first novel, changing the brother George to a sister Isabel. The death is recorded in *Stephen Hero,* the remnant of an earlier draft of *A Portrait of the Artist,* and although it is not retained in the final version of that novel, a graveyard vignette from the burial of Isabel was retained by Joyce for inclusion in the cemetery scene of *Ulysses,* poignant in its simplicity and yet purposefully gauche even in the original:

A girl, one hand catching the woman's skirt, ran a pace in advance. The girl's face was the face of a fish, discoloured and oblique-eyed; the woman's face was square and pinched, the face of a bargainer. The girl, her mouth distorted, looked up at the woman to see if it was time to cry: the woman, settling a flat bonnet, hurried towards the mortuary chapel. (*SH* 167)

In treating the sister's funeral Joyce, even in this tentative depiction, deflected the funereal mood away from the central death and introduced a detached note of painful irony. In *Ulysses* these irrelevant mourners are reduced to even further remoteness:

Mourners came out through the gates: woman and a girl. Leanjawed harpy, hard woman at a bargain, her bonnet awry. Girl's face stained with dirt and tears, holding the woman's arm looking up at her for a sign to cry. Fish's face, bloodless and livid. (*U* 101)

Stephen Dedalus's dedication toward the end of *A Portrait* in "transmuting the daily bread of experience into the radiant body of everliving life" (*AP* 221) allows for unusual metamorphoses of mundane reality. When the Dedaluses have reached a particularly low ebb in their home life, Stephen is the university student detaching himself by degrees from their poverty of home and poverty of spirit. Eating his meager breakfast of "crusts of fried bread" and "watery tea," he fingers through the pawn tickets contained in a box "speckled with lousemarks" (*AP* 174), himself dirty and lice-ridden. In *Ulysses* the Dedalus children, orphaned by the death of their mother, are the recipients of charity pea soup, pawning

Stephen's books and attempting to badger their father into donating some of the proceeds of his visits to the pawnshops. The brief glimpse into their home life reveals a kitchen redolent with the smell of shirts boiling on the stove, an even further regression down the ladder to destitution. As realistically precise as these images are in *A Portrait* and *Ulysses,* their counterpart in *Finnegans Wake* transcends the "daily bread" in comic transposition. Joyce mined a sociological study of urban blight (B. Seebohm Rowntree's *Poverty: A Study of Town Life,* 1901) and folded into the boasting of an empire builder a series of parodied quotations: "fair home overcrowded, tidy but very little furniture, respectable, whole family attends daily mass and is dead sick of bread and butter ... shares closet with eight other dwellings ... eldest son will not serve ... pays ragman in bones for faded windowcurtains ... house lost in dirt and blocked with refuse" (*FW* 543.22-33). Within the complex and all-inclusive mosaic of the *Wake* the family situation of the John Stanislaus Joyce clan during the turn-of-the-century years is minutely depicted ("serious student is eating his last dinners ... ottawark and regular loafer ... underages very treacly and verminous have to be separated ... head of domestic economy never mentioned ... as respectable as respectable can repectably be" [*FW* 544.14-545.12]).

The Young Poet

James Joyce's career as a writer dates back to his ninth year with the "publication" by his father of a poem "Et tu, Healy," proudly distributed by John Joyce to his cronies. It is somewhat ironic that Joyce, who has had a reputation as a relatively nonpolitical writer in a politically explosive era, should have begun as a political polemicist, denouncing those who betrayed Charles Stewart Parnell (after the divorce proceedings and marriage to Katharine O'Shea) and wrested the leadership of the Irish Parliamentary party from him. The child's poem is now probably irrevocably lost, but echoes of it can be found in *Finnegans Wake,* just as echoes of Parnell's career and his dramatic fall from power can be located throughout Joyce's work, from the short story "Ivy Day in the Committee Room" (a tale of Dublin petty politics eleven years to the day after Parnell's untimely death), through the highly charged Christmas dinner scene in *A Portrait* and numerous references in *Ulysses* and in the *Wake*. As an exemplar of the modernist literary movement of the early twentieth century, Joyce characteristically concerns himself primarily with the figure of the artist attaining his individual stature, yet counterpoints his lonely protagonist against a complex world that includes the Ireland of his youth and the European scene of his mature years.

With the composition of an essay that he titled "A Portrait of the Artist," written when he was twenty-one, Joyce might be said to have begun his "single" piece of literary creation, an essay-narrative which evolved into a quasi-autobiographical novel, first titled *Stephen Hero* but eventually *A Portrait of the Artist as a Young Man,* the "book of the self" that is always at the core of James Joyce's work. The poems and his surviving play *Exiles* are also a part of the singular self-involved opus, while the short stories of *Dubliners,* which track the self-figure with corresponding analogues of the world outside that self, eventually joined together in *Ulysses* and *Finnegans Wake,* the Ulyssean narrative originally intended as one more *Dubliners* story to be added on after "The Dead." These parallel courses of the highly individuated artist (whether named Stephen Daedalus—later Dedalus—or Richard Rowan or Shem the Penman) in conjunction with the ordinary citizen (various Dubliners, but essentially Leopold Bloom and H. C. Earwicker) are the directions indicated throughout the development of Joyce's body of work. The tentative "A Portrait of the Artist" approaches a Joycean aesthetic applicable to that body of work, with its insistence on a depiction of "the past" as a "fluid succession of presents" and on the liberation "from the personalised lumps of matter that which is their individuating rhythm, the first or formal relation of their parts." An important clue to the reading of *Dubliners* and *A Portrait* is the early assertion that "for such as these a portrait is not an identificative paper but rather the curve of an emotion."

It came as no surprise to James Joyce that his "Portrait" essay-narrative was rejected by the editor of *Dana*, a Dublin literary magazine at the turn of the century. Joyce saw himself at this early stage in his development moving against the grain of conventional literary taste, a rebel in his aesthetics as well as in his rejection of the Roman Catholicism of his upbringing and in his disdain for the nationalistic verse written under the pale aura of the Celtic Twilight renaissance in Irish literature. The major literary form for intellectuals in Dublin at the time was poetry, and the young writer initially viewed his own talents as those of a poet. Various influences were at work on his creative imagination, including the Romantic poets (particularly Shelley) and the Elizabethan writers of songs. In giving fictive flesh to his schooldays at Belvedere College in Dublin, Joyce presents a Stephen Dedalus in *A Portrait* staunchly defending Lord Byron against the vulgar onslaughts of the champions of Lord Tennyson in Victorian Dublin. But the only example of Stephen's own verse in the novel, apparently a youthful creation of James Joyce's that he reserviced for inclusion in *A Portrait*, is "The Villanelle of the Temptress," an exercise in fixed verse strongly redolent of Swinburne and the Pre-Raphaelites.

In *Ulysses*, written between 1915 and 1922 when Joyce, having exiled himself from Ireland, was resident in Trieste, Zurich, and Paris, Stephen is again seen replicating the young Joyce's exercises as a practicing poet. In this instance, however, the quatrain that he records is imitative to the point of unconscious plagiarism of a Douglas Hyde translation from the Irish, "My Grief on the Sea." Stephen's version reads:

> *On swift sail flaming*
> *From storm and south*
> *He comes, pale vampire,*
> *Mouth to my mouth. (U 132)*

Joyce himself had strenuously resisted the lure of the Gaelic Revival, considering the reverence for the Irish past a retrogressive movement for a nation that he dubbed "a backwash," "an afterthought of Europe," and opted instead for the influence of the European mainstream. Admiring dramatists Ibsen and Hauptmann, and such novelists as Flaubert, Tolstoi, and Henry James, he also indulged heavily in French symbolist poetry, especially Mallarmé, Rimbaud, and Verlaine, yet symbolism as such affected his narrative techniques to a far greater extent than his poetry, giving important shape to *Ulysses* in particular.

Although Joyce had essentially abandoned the idea of being a poet and was thoroughly committed to his career as a prose writer while at work on *Ulysses,* he could nonetheless recapture in his novel both the desire of a young artist to write poetry and the poetic potential of that young artist. Whereas in *A Portrait* the reader is taken through the creative process as Stephen is composing the villanelle, in *Ulysses* we are aware of the moment of inspiration, but not of the actual composition—the written result only presented hours after the writing and even then in Stephen's thoughts rather than as a transcribed manuscript. The image of the pale vampire had precipitated the desire to write, and this aspect of his dead mother remains the only truly original infusion into the Hyde quatrain. Having remembered the four lines he had written, Stephen engages in the process of dissecting the technique, essentially quarreling with Hyde's rhymed words:

Mouth, south. Is the mouth south someway? Or the south a mouth? Must be some. South, pout, out, shout, drouth. Rhymes: two men dressed the same, looking the same, two by two.

. . . . *la tua pace*
. . . . *che parlar ti piace*
. . . . *mentreché il vento, come fa, si tace.*

He saw them three by three, approaching girls, in green, in rose, in russet, entwining, *per l'aer perso* in mauve, in purple, *quella pacifica oriafiamma,* in gold of oriflamme, *di rimirar fe piu ardenti.* But I old men, penitent, leadenfooted, underdarkneath the night: mouth south: tomb womb. (*U* 138)

Not only does Stephen question the aptness of the leaden rhyme words he used, but also the limitation of mere double rhyme prosaically defined as look-alike men, when Dante Alighieri deployed his terza rima with such glowingly colorful effect. It is to Dante in the original Italian that Stephen turns, rather than to an English translation from the Irish (assuming that he is unaware of his "borrowing," although Joyce obviously is not), and in the transition from masculine English rhymes to feminine Italian rhymes he changes the gender of the look-alikes from men to women. The quatrain remains Stephen's secret creation during the course of 16 June 1904, but his reputation as a putative poet in Dublin is already extant, as is apparent when friend Lynch chides him for his claims to poetic laurels: "those leaves . . . will adorn you more fitly when something more, and greatly more, than a capful of light odes can call your genius father" (*U* 415).

As a Dublin university student Joyce had devoted serious consideration to those "odes," and involved himself in the process of structuring them into a patterned volume to be titled *Chamber Music*. Constantly arranging and rearranging, a process that would continue into the composition of the prose masterpieces, *Ulysses* and *Finnegans Wake*, Joyce sought an overall form. Even the published order of the poems has been challenged as perhaps not in line with Joyce's own preferences, but instituted by Joyce's brother Stanislaus to provide a narrative cycle somewhat more literal than Joyce's more imaginative order. Love and the disappointments of love are thematically responsible for the tone of the thirty-six poems, and they have been credited with analogy to Elizabethan lyrics, particularly those of Ben Jonson. As late as 1902, when Joyce was in Paris as a presumed medical student, he was carefully reading Jonson at the Bibliothèque Sainte-Geneviève. A year later the collection of lyrics was complete as they now stand, and Joyce sought to have them published as a book. Their lyric qualities have at times been admired, even if their poetic merits may be slight and uneven, and every one of the thirty-six pieces has been set to music many times over, some by Joyce himself.

In *Chamber Music* the poet sang his songs of innocence and experience, in a vague atmosphere of pastoral settings and quickly sketched scenes. A sense of the casual seems carefully prepared, and few poetic elements distract from the light and deft touches that give these lyrics their airy and lambent quality. The verses are kept brief, with no discernible pattern in their individual constructions: they range from a single six-line poem to several of two, three, and four stanzas, but none over eighteen lines. Most are handled in short-lined rhymes, at times with foreshortened rhyme-lines, but occasionally the reader encounters a quick change of pace with longer, more rhythmic feet, especially in the surprising onrush of the last poem, a coda to the narrative suite that precedes it. The language is studiously simple, yet many a rhyme word breaks the precedent through multisyllabic complexity. Once the winter poems of failed love and betrayed friendship become apparent toward the end of the sequence, readers can retrace their steps to recover a pattern of early springtime and vaguely summery poems at the outset, and possibly autumnal poems leading to the obvious wintriness. But, as with every other aspect of *Chamber Music,* the figures in the carpet are subtle and faint, and the poems may aptly be described as a "capful of light odes."

At a time in his youth when the shabbiness of his none-too-genteel status was painfully apparent to him and the subject of his first attempt in *Stephen Hero* of quasi-autobiographical fiction, Joyce's verses maintained a delicacy and fragility in sharp contrast to his life and his prose. During the three years between completing the collection of poems and having it accepted for publication, Joyce distanced himself from these frail, youthful indiscretions, and living in Trieste where he eked out a meager existence as a husband and father by teaching English at the Berlitz School, he had already completed the fifteen "harsh" stories of *Dubliners,* scrapped the thousand pages of *Stephen Hero,* and begun the revised version that would become *A Portrait of the Artist as a Young Man.* He was leery, therefore, of having *Chamber Music* represent his genius as his first book publication, but through the good offices of Arthur Symons, who maintained that the poems had "genuine lyric quality," they were published in London. Joyce admitted that they had "a certain grace," but insisted that a single page of one of his *Dubliners* stories "gave me more pleasure than all my verses," and he spent several hours pacing up and down the Piazza delle Poste debating with Stanislaus his resolve to cable London and retract his "dishonest" poems.

Not that Joyce the scatological ironist was entirely absent from the naive lyricism of *Chamber Music*. He circulated the anecdote that the title had been verified in its alternate sense when he overheard a demimondaine making her own kind of music into a chamber pot during an interruption of his reading of the poems to her—and took it as a good omen. Leopold Bloom in *Ulysses* contemplates just such a pun possibility, and there are references in *Finnegans Wake* to "chambermade music" and to "a period of pure lyricism of shamebred music" (*FW* 184.4,164.15-16). One critic has traced a solid vein of micturition double entendres in the volume; another has discerned a pattern of religious symbolism not unlike that of the *Portrait* villanelle; and a third has found a harbinger of stylistic concerns that were to be so prominent in the mature prose works. Of the thirty-six, the concluding poem, "I hear an army charging upon the land," has attained some degree of stature, and Joyce could be gratified by the continued acknowledgment of the musical value of his lyrics. But the essential reading of *Chamber Music* is done with a constant awareness of Joyce's major work and of Joyce biography in mind.

Joyce developed an early talent for scurrilous doggerel that he retained throughout his life, a talent that he shared with various Dublin acquaintances, especially Oliver St. John Gogarty, whose "Ballad of Joking Jesus" Joyce incorporated into the first chapter of *Ulysses*. His two most important broadsides date from 1904 and 1912, departing salvos in each instance as Joyce returned in anger and disappointment to his continental residence—the final one for the last time. "The Holy Office" is a long diatribe in rhymed couplets castigating various elements of the Dublin intelligentsia, specifying them by name and including Yeats, Synge, Æ, Gogarty, and others, and asserting a fierce independence of spirit for himself, a lone defiant mountaintop creature with flashing antlers. Originally intended for publication in Dublin while he was still living there, it was released instead after his departure and served as his poetic statement of termination of contract with his intellectual roots: "That they may dream their dreamy dreams / I carry off their filthy streams."

After a prolonged visit in 1912 Joyce departed once again in a rage against the publisher who, despite a signed contract, had finally refused to publish *Dubliners,* and on trains heading away from his native city he penned his "Gas from a Burner." As virulent a broadside as its predecessor it is nonetheless light and witty, and artfully employs the publisher himself as the persona speaking the lines of apologia in his own defense. "Gas from a Burner" is also a catalogue of the same writers cauterized in "The Holy Office," with playful variations on their names, but characterizes Joyce far more genially as

> that bloody fellow,
> That was over here dressed in Austrian yellow,
> Spouting Italian by the hour.

Irish puritanical hypocrisy and insular narrow-mindedness are the targets of Joyce's satirical venom, as he labels his Ireland, "This lovely land that always sent / Her writers and artists to banishment," and places himself within that tradition. His caustic talent for doggerel served Joyce well in *Finnegans Wake* particularly, in such set pieces as the "Ballad of Persse O'Reilly," the Hymn for Iseult la Belle, and the broadside of the Ondt and the Gracehoper. Joyce apparently detected in himself a tendency toward sentimentality that made him suspicious of the lyrics of *Chamber Music,* and he consequently overcompensated in the composition of a succession of arch verses.

He continued to write serious poetry, although infrequently, while at work on *Ulysses* and *Finnegans Wake*, and in 1927 published his only other book of verse, a sheaf of thirteen poems under the modest title of *Pomes Penyeach*, published by the Paris publisher of *Ulysses*, Sylvia Beach's Shakespeare and Company. Unlike the previous "suite" of poems that gave interlocking structures to *Chamber Music*, the later collection by a now-famous novelist contained poems that are far more individuated, each with a title of its own and none dependent upon any of the others. "Tilly," the opening poem, was actually left over from *Chamber Music*, deleted when Joyce found that it had no real place in the "suite." Most of the selections date from the Trieste years (1904-15) and carry over much of the delicate love motif that pervaded the first book, although Joyce insisted that his early love poetry was suspect because he himself was not a lover. These poems, however, are mostly understated, replete with romantic élan but steering clear of sentimentality. "She Weeps over Rahoon" is both personal in that it derives from Nora Barnacle's past experiences and extraliterary in that it corroborates the events of the novella that concludes *Dubliners*, "The Dead." And the persistence of sea imagery in the Trieste poems has its stylistic echoes in the "Proteus" chapter of *Ulysses*.

Whereas *Chamber Music* exists as the major effort of a young artist groping for his medium, *Pomes Penyeach* was published as exercises in a minor key by an accomplished master of ironic prose. Each poem is an intaglio of a captured moment, a deep but fleeting sensation, at times intensely personal and autobiographical ("A Flower given to my Daughter"), although an occasional blending of outer objectivity and inner emotion ("Bahnhofstrasse") complements the condition of a Leopold Bloom navigating the streets of an indifferent metropolis. All of the verses stay within the two- or three-stanza format, usually quatrains of simple rhyme and even simpler language, offering in poetic form a directness that differs remarkably from the language and styles of indirection operative in the prose works. Yet both volumes seem only anticipatory of the one poem that remains as Joyce's single poetic gem, "Ecce Puer," written in 1932 and often appended to later editions of *Pomes Penyeach*. The birth of his grandson Stephen Joyce soon after the death of his father John Stanislaus Joyce provided James Joyce with an emotional basis for the poem, and his insistence on a brief lyric of understatement worked ideally for the beautiful and simple piece, that concludes:

> A child is sleeping:
> An old man gone.
> O, father forsaken,
> Forgive your son!

The perfection of simplicity attained in "Ecce Puer" is not an isolated instance in Joyce's writings: most of his poems aspired toward that ideal, and facets of the poetic prose of *Ulysses* and *Finnegans Wake* achieved it as well, although in those works the *phrase juste* was often folded into the intricate texture of multiple linguistic embroideries. Stephen Dedalus's fascination with the "colour of words" persisted as Joyce's own, and he contended that a six-word sentence in *Ulysses* had required hours of work: "Perfume of embraces all him assailed" (*U* 168). The thousands of lyrical moments in *Finnegans Wake* also attest to just such poetic concerns where the language of emotional impact derives from the exactness of the contextual situation, just as when Bloom, torn between nostalgic remembrances of Molly and awareness of her impending infidelity, sees rich lingerie in a shop window and yields to the embraces of an implied "perfume." Physical hunger at the lunch hour, however, also has its sensuous intrusion, and his next thought retains the cadences of the previous sentence in an altered context: "With hungered flesh obscurely, he mutely craved to adore" (*U* 168). Poetic presence and poetic posture are never far from each other in Joyce's mature prose, the former an extension of the lyrical impulses he discerns in the human soul (Bloom's as well as Stephen's), and the latter as an essence of dramatic gesture, the tendency to adopt a role or a facade in human interexchange *Finnegans Wake* proves to be a cacophony of human voices craving to be heard, voices often assuming theatrical intonations, echoing voices of the past. In retrospect, the fifty short lyrics eventually put together as James Joyce's *Collected Poems* represent an aspect of his literary art within the larger focus of his monumental prose works.

2

The Road to *Dubliners*

Mapping the Grand Design

The Joyce who began as a writer of short pieces of lyric verse also found himself writing short pieces of prose, first in a series of what he called "epiphanies," minute anecdotes, observations, overheard conversations, and recorded dream sequences. Initially they existed as separate entities in themselves, and in *Ulysses* Stephen Dedalus treats them sardonically as remembered juvenilia, although they could not have been too far back in the past for the twenty-two-year-old unproved writer: "Remember your epiphanies on green oval leaves, deeply deep, copies to be sent if you died to all the great libraries of the world, including Alexandria? Someone was to read them there after a few thousand years, a mahamanvantara" (*U* 40). The presumed value of these fugitive pieces is undercut by Stephen's ironic tone, but the parallel exists in the Proteus chapter of *Ulysses* and the flotsam and jetsam of the shore on which Stephen walks, aware that "Signatures of all things I am here to read, seaspawn and seawrack" (*U* 37), particularized as "a damp crackling mast, razorshells, squeaking pebbles, that on the unnumbered pebbles beats, wood sieved by the shipworm, lost Armada" (*U* 40-41). Even in this juxtaposition Joyce retains an awareness of the complex relationship of the trivial with the vital, the minutiae which reflects all of history, the signatures that are emblematic for the text: "Books you were going to write with letters for titles. Have you read his F? O yes, but I prefer Q. Yes, but W is wonderful. O yes, W" (*U* 40). And in his own mind, as is particularly demonstrated in Proteus, the flotsam and jetsam of his intellect, education, and emotional reactions are as randomly strewn, demanding the structuring skills of the mature artist.

In *Stephen Hero* he had set great store for his epiphanic observations. Not only had "a trivial incident set him composing some ardent verses" (*SH* 211), but the scheme for collecting the elements of incidental life is given further justification:

This triviality made him think of collecting such moments together in a book of epiphanies. By an epiphany he meant a sudden spiritual manifestation, whether in the vulgarity of speech or of gesture or in a memorable phase of the mind itself. He believed that it was for the man of letters to record these epiphanies with great care, seeing that they themselves are the most delicate and evanescent of moments. He told Cranly that the clock of the Ballast Office was capable of an epiphany. Cranly questioned the inscrutable dial of the Ballast Office with his no less inscrutable countenance:
—Yes, said Stephen. I will pass it time after time, allude to it, refer to it, catch a glimpse of it. It is only an item in the catalogue of Dublin's street furniture. Then all at once I see it and I know at once what it is: epiphany. (*SH* 211)

Joyce harvested several dozen of these epiphanies, never completely discarding them as he developed his larger prose works but folding a handful of them into *Stephen Hero* itself. When he abandoned that unfinished novel, he retained the image of the woman and daughter at the funeral for the Hades chapter of *Ulysses,* and built an even more evanescent structure from it as that text developed. The two isolated figures are only casually observed by Bloom as he enters Glasnevin for Dignam's interment; they are on their way out, and it is in his focus of contemplation that certain details are registered and retained. When in a Circe "hallucination" Bloom is credited with encountering the grieving Mrs. Dignam and her brood of children, he has since visited the widow and presumably seen her children there as well, but the Circe "incident" offers the first description of the family:

(Mrs Dignam, widow woman, her snubbed nose and cheeks flushed with deathtalk, tears and Tunny's tawny sherry, hurries by in her weeds, her bonnet awry, rouging and powdering her cheeks, lips and nose, a pen chivvying her brood of cygnets. Beneath her skirt appear her late husband's everyday trousers and turnedup boots, large eights. She holds a Scottish widow's insurance policy and large marqueeumbrella under which her brood runs with her, Patsy hopping on one short foot, his collar loose, a hank of porksteaks dangling, Freddy whimpering, Susy with a crying cod's mouth, Alice struggling with the baby. She cuffs them on, her streamers flaunting aloft.) (U 568)

Allowing for the magic transformations of the Circean experience, the details of this family portrait probably owe a great deal to Bloom's hour or two spent at the Dignam residence working out the difficulties of the insurance, yet it is not likely that he saw Mrs. Dignam indoors with her hat on. Instead, he has transferred the image of the woman at Glasnevin with *her bonnet awry,* and added to Susy a close variant of the daughter's *fish's face* as a *crying cod's mouth.* Neither the widow nor her daughter Susy was present at Paddy Dignam's interment, an all-male occasion carefully enumerated and catalogued, so that Bloom has had an unconscious epiphany of the woman and daughter and made an unconscious transfer based on the evanescent moment. The superimposition of a recuperated experience upon a new and similar context becomes the accretive process of the development of *Ulysses,* and mirrors the superimposing of autobiographic and recorded details by Joyce upon the fictional texts. Several epiphanies make the journey from the "green oval leaves" into *Stephen Hero* and eventually into *A Portrait*

of the Artist as well, where they blend into a format replete
with numerous evanescent moments. Whereas the early
"Apologise" vignette is taken from a preexisting epiphany, its
later counterparts in "Admit" are newly constructed for the
situations evolving in *A Portrait* and have the same epiphanic
impact. Epiphanies as separate and discrete texts may have
been discarded by their creator, but the essence of the concept
was retained throughout his novels.

The first short stories that Joyce wrote and published were
hardly more extensive than the epiphanies he collected,
although their eventual collection in the *Dubliners* volume
gives the impression of a sustained and extensive prose work.
Concurrent with his presumed vocation as a poet he availed
himself of whatever opportunities presented themselves in
paid publication, and offered three of the stories that would
become the nucleus of *Dubliners* to the *Irish Homestead,* a
journal edited by George Russell (and referred to in *Ulysses* as
the "pig's paper" [U 193]). The limitations of that format
dictated that the stories be extremely short, straightforward,
simple, and easily comprehensible (hardly Joycean characteristics), but for the minimal remuneration and while the
offer lasted Joyce provided acceptable examples of the genre.
By 1904 he had decided to develop the vignettes and expand
them into a collection of what he called "epicleti"—ten of
them to form a comprehensive volume. By the time he first
offered the volume to a publisher in April 1905 it had
expanded to twelve stories, and a structuring pattern had been
imposed on them: three stories each on children, young adults,
mature adults, and public life. (The James Joyce who habitually
thought in terms of patterns and structures was now in full
control of his material.) Within another year he enhanced the
pattern to include two more tales, one in the section on young
adults and one in the section on mature adults, but a basic
symmetry was preserved in the balance of three/four/
four/three. The stories were intensified and carefully
resculpted, and among the various apologiae for them Joyce
inserted a note on the style of "scrupulous meanness" exerted

in their execution. On the surface they retained an apparent aspect of simplicity, but they were far from random selections of Dublin life, especially since Joyce advertised them to his prospective publishers as a "moral chapter of the history" of Ireland, citing the city of Dublin as the "centre of paralysis."

The frustrating years between the first acceptance for publication of *Dubliners* and its eventual appearance in 1914 constituted the second stage of Joyce's maturation as a literary artist and a fierce entrenchment of his determination to be uncompromising in his art. By 1907 he added a long coda story to *Dubliners,* at a crucial time in his life and his career when he was also abandoning the comprehensive *Stephen Hero* for work on the economically honed *Portrait of the Artist,* and although "The Dead" seems out of proportion and even out of kilter with the rest of *Dubliners,* that novella in many ways recapitulates many of the themes and patterns of the preceding fourteen stories and carries the collection into a further dimension. That Joyce later contemplated an additional story to be called "Ulysses" for the book seems even more peculiar, especially when we become aware that the germ for that story matured into the enormous novel of that title. But the battle over publication of these "controversial" tales exerted its impact on their author, and it must have rankled Joyce to have to "stand still" in his creative development.

For all its expansiveness as a cross section of his city around the turn of the century, *Dubliners* proves to be a highly limited approach to material available to James Joyce. His focus is almost exclusively on the middle-class Catholic Dubliners within his own and his father's circle of acquaintances, since by his own admission Joyce maintained that he never could "invent" fictional material. Within the confines of the dominant element of the social structure of Dublin, however, he managed to work out numerous variations and combinations: among the Dublin Catholic bourgeoisie an occasional ex-Protestant can be seen backsliding a bit in "Grace," and a practicing Protestant is apparent at the Christmastide festivities among his Catholic neighbors in "The Dead." And "Grace" also alludes to a Dublin Jew, one of that very small community in the city at the time, which Joyce would concentrate on further in *Ulysses*. As for the economic levels of these middle-class denizens of Dublin, the range in Joyce's stories is extensive: shopgirl, law office clerk, bank employee, the scion of a wealthy butcher, and the shiftless son of a police official, as well as those living on meager incomes. The occasional workman is glimpsed in "Two Gallants" and the suggestion of wealth is apparent in "After the Race," but essentially *Dubliners* presents the common denominations of basic petty bourgeoisie.

The first three stories, "The Sisters," "An Encounter," "Araby," are not only about childhood but also told through the first-person narration of a child, a young boy who may be assumed to remain the same protagonist in the progression of stories or a separate protagonist in each. Anonymous, with no specific age designated for him, and ostensibly parentless (he lives with an aunt and uncle in "The Sisters" and "Araby"), he undergoes a series of somewhat traumatic experiences, well within the framework of ordinary childhood occurrences: the death of a priest who had served as his mentor, a run-in with a menacing stranger when out on a day's truancy from school, and the disappointment during a period of immature love when he arrives belatedly at a church bazaar where he had hoped to buy a gift. In each case the effect on the boy is measured by his own narrative, the immediacy recorded by the limited perception of an intelligent but nonetheless inexperienced and susceptible consciousness. As his aunt gossips with the priest's sisters at the side of the coffin, the boy is expected to be registering bewilderment and betrayal about the cleric's presumed madness, but the method of narration only allows for the recording of the actual conversation without registering the boy's reactions. When encountering the presumed pederast he attempts several childish ploys for his own protection against something he cannot really comprehend, but finds himself somewhat envious of his companion, a boy he considers duller than himself but who proves far more impervious to the present danger, and as they escape, the protagonist feels compelled to acknowledge: "I was penitent; for in my heart I had always despised him a little." And when he nurtures what he considers an inviolably pure love for the slightly older girl, envisioning himself as a chivalric knight carrying his chalice through a corrupt world, he finds himself at a sordidly ordinary bazaar that he had assumed would be exotic, among banal customers and flirtatious shopgirls, with insufficient funds for a real present. The intensity of his disappointment is registered in his self-denunciation as "a creature driven and derided by vanity, and my eyes burned with anguish and anger." Greater self-awareness and articulation become apparent as the boy matures through this progression of meaningful events, and the temptation to read the stories as cumulative pays richer dividends.

From the fourth story on in *Dubliners* the method of narration changes to the impersonal third person as the focus changes from childhood to the adult world, a loss of the honest immediacy of the immature perceiver and a shift to the calculated responses of the adult, but fused through an "objective" reproduction of events. "Eveline," "After the Race," "Two Gallants," and "The Boarding House," however, deal with the inexperience of what Joyce termed adolescence, although the ages of the four protagonists range from nineteen to early thirties. Each of them is trapped in the paralytic condition of the lives fashioned about them, despite the numerous differences in their individual situations. Eveline Hill is already on the eve of her departure from Dublin with a sailor-lover who is taking her to Argentina, yet her eagerness to leave her tyrannical father and depressing job fails to take account of the strength of her obligation to her dead mother to care for the young children of the family, and at the gate to the ship Eveline is physically unable to take the important step to freedom. Her impoverished background and her impoverishment of spirit contrast sharply with the wealth and élan of a Jimmy Doyle, who in "After the Race" finds himself in the exciting world of foreign auto racers, sophisticated drinkers, and gamblers, quite unaware how much he is out of his element until the all-night carousal ends in his having lost a substantial sum of money, perhaps his entire patrimony. Few of Joyce's Dubliners begin with so great a financial advantage, and few fall from such exalted financial heights: in "Two Gallants" Lenehan and Corley are unemployed loungers, although Corley's father is a police official, and his mysterious assignation with a servant girl leaves Lenehan wandering aimlessly and dejectedly through Dublin, until Corley reappears with the proceeds of his adventure, a half sovereign stolen by the slavey that will provide the gallants with drinking money. The irresponsibility of their lives is set against the seriousness of Bob Doran, gainfully employed and living in a boardinghouse where he has been seduced by the proprietor's daughter, and now faces the distasteful prospect of marrying her against his will and better judgment, terrified of losing his job because of scandal.

The mature protagonists of the next quartet of narratives, "A Little Cloud," "Counterparts," "Clay," and "A Painful Case," extend the possibilities potential in the lives of the previous four, but with no further positive development. Thomas Chandler of "A Little Cloud" is basically the same age as Lenehan and Bob Doran, and apparently as securely employed as the latter, but already married and the father of an infant son. He dreams of being a poet and expanding his horizon, and on this particular evening has drinks with an old acquaintance, a raffish journalist now with the London press, but Chandler's sensibilities are disquieted by Gallaher's coarse bragging and he retreats home to read Byron, only to be defeated by his child's wailing and his wife's anger. His counterpart is a clerk named Farrington, a family man apparently unsuited to his sedentary job, who runs afoul of his employer by his indolence and insolence. Pawning his watch for a night's carousal, Farrington is bested in hand wrestling by an English artiste and runs through his money, failing to get sufficiently drunk. Frustrated and resentful, he takes out his aggression on his son when he arrives home to find that the kitchen fire has been allowed to go out. These two married men give way to two unmarried protagonists: in "Clay" Maria leaves the laundry where she is employed for a Halloween visit to the family of Joe Donnelly, for whom she has served as a surrogate mother. Her innocence and simple-minded naiveté prevent her from realizing the hollowness and pathos of her empty life, as she is tricked by the neighbor's children into choosing the symbol of death in a game of divination. Her precarious existence is contrasted with the solid security of James Duffy of "A Painful Case," a bachelor who has insulated himself from all unpleasant contacts with other people by living alone and dependent only on his own resources. A casual friendship with a married woman, however, almost disturbed his stability, and he had precipitously terminated it before emotional involvement became too apparent. Now he finds in a newspaper item that she has drunkenly been killed or committed suicide, and the horror of her death becomes increasingly more obvious to him—along with the emptiness of his own life.

The shift to public life in "Ivy Day in the Committee Room," "A Mother," and "Grace" ostensibly expands the focus of these fuller narratives beyond concentration on a single protagonist, but in actuality a central character persists as dominant in at least the last two of the triad. More importantly, "Dubliners" in general prove to be communal protagonists, especially in "Ivy Day," where a handful of political canvassers wander into their headquarters in cold, rainy weather, discussing the politics of the day, as well as of the past, when Charles Stewart Parnell was their "uncrowned king" and leader, although the eleven years since his death have devastated their loyalties and enthusiasms. The ghost of Parnell as such dominates the committee room, and all of the petty politicos are viewed in relation to the dead leader. In "A Mother" music replaces politics as another public concern in Dublin, but disappointing attendance at a series of concerts necessitates cutting expenses on the part of the officiating committee, which attempts to renege on payment to the

accompanist, a young woman whose career is being
orchestrated by her mother. The ensuing tensions and flare-up
result in Mrs. Kearney whisking her daughter Kathleen out of
the auditorium in mid-concert, seriously affecting her future
career in Dublin. The degraded state of Irish politics and the
depleted enthusiasm for culture in Dublin are then reflected in
the condition of Irish Catholicism in "Grace," a tale of
presumed spiritual redemption. But Tom Kernan is a
backsliding Protestant who married into the Catholic faith,
and when he drunkenly falls and bites off a piece of his tongue,
his good-Samaritan Catholic friends quietly lure him into
attending a retreat for worldly businessmen, at which a Jesuit
preacher sets up a double-entry bookkeeping system for
virtues and sins. This variant of simony is the most potent in
Dubliners, where the selling of that which is sacred is an
important theme, beginning with the desire of the paralytic
Father Flynn in "The Sisters" to school the young boy into the
priesthood in which he himself has been disappointed. The
boy, fascinated by portentous words, professes an interest in
the words *paralysis, simony,* and *gnomon,* words that have
thematic reverberations throughout the ensuing stories.

The placing of "The Dead" at the end of this progression of
balanced tales is anomalous in that it is a novella far longer
than any of the others, and presumably outside the sequence.
Joyce had confessed when the fourteen stories existed as the
completed volume that his stories were somewhat harsh, and
that they failed to include the Irish talent for hospitality. "The
Dead," consequently, is a Christmas story at which family and
friends of the two spinster sisters, Kate and Julia Morkan, and
their niece Mary Jane, gather for music, dancing, feasting, and
drinking. The "sudden spiritual manifestation" of an epiphany
may have a literal understructure in "The Dead," since the
festive Christmas soirée apparently takes place several days
after the new year, probably on the very day of the Epiphany,
Twelfth Night, and the protagonist, the old women's nephew
Gabriel Conroy, is the logical recipient of that manifestation. A
teacher and critic of literature, he considers himself

intellectually above the other guests, as he prepares his after-dinner speech and toast, and as the husband of the "country-cute" Gretta he fancies himself still as an ardent lover after ten years of marriage. The conversation at the soirée is so often about the past and the dead, of forgotten singers and monks sleeping in their coffins, and toward the end of the evening Gretta succumbs nostalgically to the singing of a ballad that reminds her of a young boy who many years before had loved her and died. As the Conroys settle into their hotel room for the night, Gretta confesses to her husband for the first time that a Michael Furey had once died "for her," a passion obviously far greater than any the stolidly bourgeois Gabriel had ever himself acknowledged. As Gretta falls asleep, Gabriel broods quietly at the window watching the snow fall, perhaps aware of his own limitations, his pomposity, and his comfortable complacency. At his aunts' he had had a slight unpleasantness with a young woman who was a fervent Irish nationalist and refused an invitation to take his holidays in the West of Ireland, despite Gretta's yearning to return to her native Galway. Now at the hotel window he muses over the snow falling on Michael Furey's grave, of the imminent death of his aged aunt, of snow falling on "all the living and the dead."

The Figures in the Carpet

The positioning of the three words *paralysis, gnomon,* and *simony* in the opening paragraph of "The Sisters" sets into motion a series of thematic counters that Joyce can play for infinite and intricate variations. As the protagonist of the story articulates their magic for him at the time, they represent concepts just outside his present range of awareness, but ones with which he is on the verge of encounter and comprehension:

Every night as I gazed up at the window I said softly to myself the word *paralysis*. It had always sounded strangely in my ears, like the word *gnomon* in the Euclid and the word *simony* in the Catechism. But now it sounded to me like the name of some maleficent and sinful being. It filled me with fear, and yet I longed to be nearer to it and to look upon its deadly work. (*D* 9)

The two previous words had solid positions within frames of reference, Euclid and the Catechism, forms of educational experience germane to the boy's status as a student, an initiate into codified learning supervised by teachers. The new word has no referential context in prescribed texts, but looms frighteningly out of an uncharted world of reality that the boy must confront without the assistance of a guide. He senses that words are animate, human, alive—and consequently dangerous—yet resists shrinking from active encounter with them. Instead he finds himself fascinated and therefore committed: to look upon the "deadly work" of real life and listen to the strange sounds of its words constitute the opening approach of the artist-initiate.

The pattern in *Dubliners* develops from the literal to the metaphoric. In "The Sisters" poor Father Flynn suffers from his paralytic illness and at the age of sixty-five dies of his third paralytic stroke. That his life was a "disappointed" one, calling into question his vocation as a priest, compounds the paralysis beyond the literal physical condition into several extended ramifications. The dead priest lying in his coffin is oddly replicated by the inanimate young girl in "Eveline": she is never seen in any state other than the completely inert, although during the ellipsis between sitting at her window and standing at the railing at the North Wall docks Eveline Hill had made the transition from one place to another. Yet the only Eveline we witness in the story is either in one paralytic state or the other ("Her time was running out but she continued to sit by the window"; "She gripped with both hands at the iron railing" [*D* 39, 41]—her only movement occurs as a fleeting transition ("She stood up in a sudden impulse of terror" [*D* 40]), a trauma of paralytic arrest. Such moments of paralytic stroke are far from infrequent in *Dubliners:* in "After the Race," a tale of feverish and nervous energy, Jimmy Doyle experiences his terminal shock when Villona announces, "Daybreak, gentlemen!" just as Doyle had surrendered to a "dark stupor": "He leaned his elbows on the table and rested his head between his hands, counting the beats of his temples"

(*D* 48). The "stroke" contrast sharply with the paralytic state, but together they encapsulate the Dublin situation.

The manifestations of what Joyce called Dublin's "hemiplegia of the will" are varied throughout *Dubliners:* Eveline's inability to escape has been shown to preexist her condition as a "helpless animal" (*D* 41) at the port barrier, dating from her mother's dying words of "final craziness" (*D* 40) that had frozen Eveline in static inactivity. Jimmy Doyle's excited activity, from auto racing to whirlwind gambling, ultimately brings him to a static moment of irreparable loss. In "Two Gallants" Lenehan is in almost constant motion as he circumnavigates the streets of Dublin, but aimless and circular in his wanderings, paralytically enclosed in his penury and lack of motivation, just as Farrington in "Counterparts" moves from pub to pub until time and money run out and he is fixed in a catatonic moment of entrapment. Meaningless and illusory movement is also apparent in "Clay," where Maria traverses the length of Dublin by tram, only to confront the image of her imminent death; in "A Painful Case," where Mr. Duffy has carefully contained his world on an axis between his job in Dublin and his residence in Chapelizod, only to realize that he is irrevocably possessed by the death of Mrs. Sinico; and in "The Dead," where Gabriel considers himself a free agent, able to take his vacations on the Continent and roam Dublin at will, from his dwelling in Monkstown to his aunts' soirée in Usher's Island to temporary refuge in the Gresham Hotel—only to find that the ghost of Michael Furey traps him in his hotel room, where his only recourse is to gaze out of his window at the falling snow, realizing that the "snow was general all over Ireland" (*D* 223).

Although these movements are understated in the narratives, Joyce's method of casual presentation suggesting a veneer of generally normal activity, they are actually the desperate avenues of escape for the trapped denizens of Dublin, and derive from the efforts made by the young boy in the opening stories to locate a world outside his particular confines. In "The Sisters" he is translated by his aunt from his own home to the death house of the priest, but in "An Encounter" and "Araby" he attempts to find a haven, although temporary, from his home confinement in the lure of the Pigeon House and the Araby Bazaar—the first never attained and the second a disappointment. Eveline takes her prison with her to the docks, and her life will be permanently circumscribed between her father's house with its dusty rooms and the Stores where she is employed. Farrington's life will be further limited since his job at Crosbie and Alleyne is now seriously in jeopardy, while Maria, whose life at the Dublin by Lamplight laundry was limited enough, faces an even more impending death. A single adventure of momentary escape, whether a day's truancy or a night's carousal, a Halloween trek or a Christmas party, is only an illusion of liberated activity. Chandler in "A Little Cloud" entertains the most extreme hope of freedom, even more ambitious than Eveline Hill's thwarted prospect of married life in Buenos Aires, since he so elaborately over-poeticizes:

He stepped onward bravely.
   Every step brought him nearer to London, farther from his own sober inartistic life. A light began to tremble on the horizon of his mind. (*D* 73)

Despite the wild expectations, Little Chandler carries his sobriety with him, frustrating his potential for a Gallaher-like escape, just as Farrington indulged in temporary drunkenness, ruining his chance of retaining his sober employment. In "The Boarding House" Bob Doran, like Mr. Duffy, knows enough to be relatively content with his lot, gainfully employed and happily settled, and does not wander out in search of adventure or escape. Instead he finds entrapment waiting for him in his own dwelling, the sexual allures of Polly Mooney and the demands for marriage made by her mother and backed up by her bullying brother.
   Paralysis is as general in Joyce's *Dubliners* as snow in "The Dead" is over Ireland, and in the three stories of public life that

follow the eleven "case histories" of individual Dubliners, a facet of the general paralytic condition is scrupulously examined. The individuals of the previous stories run the gamut of possibilities, yet for each the result remains basically the same. Whether their ambitions are modest or expansive, they are disappointed; if they struggle against their bonds, they only succeed in tightening them; and if they avoid any effort at all (and Duffy is as purposely inert a character as can be imagined), they only find themselves that much more aware of the emptiness of their lives. In "Ivy Day" the political canvassers are as seedy a lot as their politics, each hamstrung by poverty, meanness, frustration, emptiness, and the political situation stultified by the loss of ideals or the hope of success. (The obviously inevitable election of Tierney neither advances the cause of Parnell nor enhances the prospects of his ward heelers.) In "A Mother" the empty concert hall and the paucity of the artistes mirror the hopes of a Kathleen Kearney for a musical career in a city in which men make their self-serving decisions over their whiskeys, committees attempt to cut their business losses by cutting out helpless females, and righteously indignant mothers contribute to the destructive condition by insisting vociferously on a regress of grievances and standing on principles. Individual cases reflect the general situation, as in "Grace," where Tom Kernan's habitual drunkenness stirs a well-intentioned trio of comforters into luring the lukewarm Catholic convert into a businessman's retreat at a Jesuit church. Kernan's comatose condition, whether drunkenly inert at the bottom of the lavatory steps or convalescent in his encircled bed, is corroborated rather than cured by the sermon of Father Purdon that takes into consideration that for them "Jesus Christ was not a hard taskmaster" and "setting before them as exemplars in the religious life those very worshippers of Mammon who were of all men the least solicitous in matters religious" (*D* 174). In the culminating story of "The Dead," politics, music, and religion, despite the festiveness of the Christmas season and the graciousness of the hospitality, are dead-ended: Gabriel is irked by the activist Molly Ivors into petulantly contending that "Irish is not my language" and "I'm sick of my own country, sick of it!" (D 189); Mary Jane plays her "Academy piece" that no one listens to (D 186) and Bartell D'Arcy is too hoarse to sing; and monks are commended for sleeping in their coffins, to the incomprehensible amazement of the Protestant guest.

As the word paralysis assumes its "maleficent and sinful" significance in "The Sisters" (to reverberate through every aspect of *Dubliners*), the word simony emerges from its safe existence in the Catechism into the fearful world of the boy's dream—and beyond. The association between paralysis and simony is made almost immediately, if somewhat inadvertently, as the boy reacts to Father Flynn's death:

In the dark of my room I imagined that I saw again the heavy grey face of the paralytic. I drew the blankets over my head and tried to think of Christmas. But the grey face still followed me. It murmured; and I understood that it desired to confess something. I felt my soul receding into some pleasant and vicious region; and there again I found it waiting for me. It began to confess to me in a murmuring voice and I wondered why it smiled continually and why the lips were so moist with spittle. But then I remembered that it had died of paralysis and I felt that I too was smiling feebly as if to absolve the simoniac of his sin. (D 11)

The relationship of the boy and the priest who had been his mentor has troubled readers of "The Sisters," and the complications are compounded by the inexperienced child as the sole source of narration, especially since he ceases to respond openly to his experiences in the latter part of the story. In recording his "dream" (it is only later that he refers to these images of revery as part of a dream) he understandably hides behind certain protective screens (the priest's face referred to impersonally as "it") and has no way of indicating why he has reversed roles with the Father Confessor, why he should assume the priest to have committed simony, or why—if he himself is the actual simoniac—he should accuse himself of simony.

That Father Flynn may have "had a great wish" for the boy, and that he was a "disappointed man" whose "life was, you might say, crossed" (*D* 10, 17), suggests that the priest sought to pass on his vocation to the boy despite his own misgivings, perhaps an aspect of simony that the recipient in some way sensed. There are, oddly enough, few other representatives of the Catholic priesthood in *Dubliners,* and several of those are also suspect: Father Butler in "An Encounter" is a stern schoolmaster, with no other role in the story except as the disciplinarian, but "An Encounter" is a narrative in which it is disclosed that schoolboy Joe Dillon, who played fiercely as a Wild West Indian, is destined to become a priest: "Everyone was incredulous when it was reported that he had a vocation for the priesthood. Nevertheless it was true" (*D* 19). The boy in "Araby" lives in a house in which a priest "had died in the back drawing-room" (*D* 29), and Gabriel Conroy's brother Constantine is "senior curate in Balbriggan" (*D* 186), but inexplicably absent from the Christmas party at his aunts'. In "Ivy Day" a Father Burke is mentioned as a supporter of the candidate, and an even more mysterious cleric makes a furtive appearance: "A person resembling a poor clergyman or a poor actor appeared in the doorway" (*D* 125), a Father Keon who never quite states his business, except to say that he is looking for the subsheriff, and becomes the source of gossip once he leaves. ("I think he's what you call a black sheep," Mr. Henchy reports; "He's an unfortunate man of some kind" [*D* 126]). And in "Grace" the Jesuit Father Purdon establishes his spiritual cash register for the worldly men of business.

Simony translates itself in *Dubliners* in secular terms more often than religious, in every aspect of the buying and selling of things sacrosanct, as a form of betrayal of fellow humans and of human values, and often for precise monetary exchanges. The boy in "The Sisters" remains relatively untainted by the exchange of money: he bears the "gift" of snuff to the priest from his aunt (possibly in exchange for lessons), and is aware that sherry and biscuits are "offered" at the wake, and that flowers were brought by Father O'Rourke and candles lent from the chapel. A system of barter, donation, and charity prevails as yet in his young life, and his knowledge that Old Cotter was once connected with a distillery means "faints and worms" to him, rather than an occupation (*D* 10). His is a world in which Father Flynn's life is bartered for an "eternal reward" (*D* 16), and although he might still be unaware of the exact price of a packet of snuff, he will eventually learn that money is needed for a day's "miching" and how much a ticket to the Araby Bazaar will actually cost. The three schoolboys in "An Encounter" contribute sixpence each for the day away from school, the sum held in surety by the protagonist, and when Leo Dillon fails to appear, Mahony insists that Dillon's share is "forfeit"—"And so much the better for us—a bob and a tanner instead of a bob" (*D* 22). Without demur his cohort accepts the windfall, taking for himself his friend's money. In "Araby" he is dependent on his uncle's largesse, only to realize that the florin is insufficient to buy a gift impressive enough for Mangan's sister. Whether he is ever aware that he had hoped to purchase her favor with his uncle's florin, he is nonetheless thwarted by the inadequacy of the sum and the tawdriness of the bazaar, and he views himself "as a creature driven and derided by vanity; and my eyes burned with anguish and anger" (*D* 35).

When Farrington determines upon an evening of "truancy"—"he must have a good night's drinking" (*D* 87)—he finds himself penniless, and pawns his watch for six shillings, after having been offered only five: "He came out of the pawn-office joyfully, making a little cylinder of the coins between his thumb and fingers" (*D* 93). But he buys more drinks for others than he succeeds in garnering for himself and spends a pathetically disappointing evening in the pubs, without even getting drunk. When he returns home, he confronts his young son Tom and proceeds to beat him; the terrified child desperately hopes to stave off further punishment by offering up prayers for his father:

—O, pa! he cried. Don't beat me, pa! and I'll . . . I'll say a *Hail Mary* for you. . . . I'll say a *Hail Mary* for you, pa, if you don't beat me. . . . I'll say a *Hail Mary*. . . . (*D* 98)

The boy has already learned that there is a possible "currency" in the insincere prayer, and is willing to barter it for escape from punishment.

Adults with actual money to offer are more successful than the pathetic Tom Farrington. In "The Dead" Gabriel Conroy views himself as imbued with the spirit of Christmas; after all, he had lent Freddy Malins a pound ("at Christmas," he tells his wife, "when he opened that little Christmas-card shop in Henry Street" [*D* 217])—a gesture that earns him not only the return of his money, but also a kiss from his wife ("—You are a very generous person, Gabriel, she said" [*D* 217]). But when Gabriel finds himself in an embarrassing conversation with the servant girl Lily, suddenly aware that he had committed a gaucherie in treating the young woman as an inexperienced schoolgirl, he quickly covers his embarrassment with a proferred coin:

Then he took a coin rapidly from his pocket.
—O Lily, he said, thrusting it into her hands, it's Christmas-time, isn't it? Just . . . here's a little. . . .
    He walked rapidly towards the door. (*D* 178)

The money covered the first embarrassment for him, and Christmas is offered as an excuse to cover the further embarrassment.

In "Clay" it is a prayer book rather than a coin that serves the ulterior purpose. Maria on All-Hallowed Eve journeys across Dublin to visit the family of Joe Donnelly, for whom she had once served as a surrogate mother, and brings cakes for the festivities. An aging spinster working at a charity laundry, she is already aware that there is no real home for her at the Donnellys': "Often he had wanted her to go and live with them; but she would have felt herself in the way (though Joe's wife was ever so nice with her) and she had become accustomed to the life of the laundry" (*D* 100), but she is looking forward to the party, with "all the children singing!" (*D* 100). At the party, however, she is made the unwitting victim of a childish prank:

They led her up to the table amid laughing and joking and she put her hand out in the air as she was told to do. She moved her hand about here and there in the air and descended on one of the saucers. She felt a soft wet substance with her fingers and was surprised that nobody spoke or took off her bandage. There was a pause for a few seconds; and then a great deal of scuffling and whispering. Somebody said something about the garden, and at last Mrs Donnelly said something very cross to one of the next-door girls and told her to throw it out at once: that was no play. Maria understood that it was wrong that time and so she had to do it over again; and this time she got the prayer-book. (*D* 105)

Intimations of death follow the indications that there is no life for Maria at the Donnellys', and the prayer book is quickly introduced as an appeasement.

The prayer book serves as an odd simoniac instance; usually it is a coin of the realm that signifies the buying of something that should not be sold: a forfeited sixpence, an inadequate florin, a small coin tendered to cover an embarrassment, a crown offered as a loan for a watch. But no single coin glistens as persuasively in *Dubliners* as Corley's triumphantly revealed half sovereign in "Two Gallants." Whatever the reader's suspicions are regarding Corley's quest and Lenehan's attendant anxieties, the revelation of the gold coin in his palm illuminated under the lamplight is a major shock as Corley makes his grandiose gesture of triumph: "he extended a hand towards the light and, smiling, opened it slowly to the gaze of his disciple. A small gold coin shone in the palm" (*D* 60). In an instance the significance of a night's drinking, the seduction and debasement of the domestic servant, the stealing from her employer—all the demeaning and dishonest acts are highly illuminated as the extension of simony into everyday life in Dublin.

That life is constantly depicted in *Dubliners* as characteristic of a society paralyzed by the absence of a redeeming spirit: priests are dead or missing, or themselves devoid of the holy spirit. "You couldn't tell when the breath went out of him," says his sister of Father Flynn (*D* 15), and when Leo Dillon worries that they might encounter Father Butler during their day of truancy, "Mahony asked, very sensibly, what would Father Butler be doing out at the Pigeon House" (*D* 21). The various symbolic coinages of the Holy Spirit are manifest throughout *Dubliners*, as bird, as flame, as tongue, as a rush of air: Father O'Rourke (in Hebrew *ruach* means air or spirit) had intended hiring an automobile "at Johnny Rush's" to take Father Flynn on an outing to Irishtown, where he was born, an automobile that Eliza Flynn says has "rheumatic wheels" (*D* 17)—an absence of *pneuma* (Greek for air or spirit). The quest for the Pigeon House, the sanctuary of the Holy Dove, is never achieved in "An Encounter," but Mahony has brought along a slingshot, "to have some gas with the birds. Mahony used slang freely, and spoke of Father Butler as Bunsen Burner" (*D* 22). In "The Dead" the Protestant Mr. Browne is reported by Kate Morkan to have been "laid on here like the gas . . . all during the Christmas" (*D* 206), and Michael Furey is reported by Gretta Conroy to have been "in the gasworks" (*D* 219). Gabriel, on entering the hotel room, rejects the offer of a candle ("We don't want any light. We have light enough from the street"—but that proves to be a "ghostly light from the street lamp" [*D* 216]), a reminder that backsliding Tom Kernan, who had bitten off a bit of his tongue in his "fall from grace" and consequently speaks indistinctly—if not quite "in tongues," had his serious objection to having a candle at the Jesuit retreat: "I bar the candles, said Mr. Kernan . . . I bar the magic-lantern business" (*D* 171). *"For the children of this world are wiser in their generation than the children of light,"* begins the text of Father Purdon's sermon, and *Dubliners* is distinctly marked by the absence of the children of light (*D* 173).

In the "style of scrupulous meanness" adopted by Joyce for his *Dubliners* many connectives, climaxes, and resolutions are often missing, attesting to the definition of the gnomon in Euclidian geometry: "the remainder of a parallelogram after the removal of a similar parallelogram containing one of its corners" (the word coming from the Greek for an interpreter, the pointer on a sundial). The stories in Joyce's volume are intended to be read by understanding the substance from the shadow it casts, or intimating the shadow from the substance. Even before he makes the association between the Euclidian word with the other two words, the boy explains that

Night after night I had passed the house (it was vacation time) and studied the lighted square of window; and night after night I had found it lighted in the same way, faintly and evenly. If he was dead, I thought, I would see the reflection of candles on the darkened blind for I knew that two candles must be set at the head of a corpse. (*D* 9)

The boy attempts to "read" the "lighted square," assuming that the added dimension of the reflected candles would cast their informative shadow for him, but is disappointed. Instead the news of the priest's death is transmitted by Old Cotter when the boy comes down to supper, so that what once was a condition contrary to fact ("If he was dead") now becomes a fact, and Cotter's "unfinished sentences" (*D* 11) are heavy with gnomonic ellipses: "No, I wouldn't say he was exactly . . . but there was something queer . . . there was something uncanny about him. I'll tell you my opinion." (*D* 9-10). The next day the boy returns to the priest's house, and now missing is the notice that "used to hang in the window, saying: *Umbrellas Recovered.* No notice was visible now for the shutters were up" (*D* 11). Instead, there is a card informing of the death of Father Flynn, and that he was "formerly of S. Catherine's Church" (*D* 12), and this time the boy transposes the condition contrary to fact: "Had he not been dead I would have gone into the little dark room" (*D* 12). When he does visit the corpse, he can only pretend to pray, and fancies "that the old priest was smiling as he lay there in his coffin" (*D* 14)—the mere ghost of a smile—and his last glimpse corroborates the *presence* of the body that initimates a corresponding absence: "there was no sound in the house: and I knew that the old priest was lying still in his coffin as we had seen him, solemn and truculent in death, an idle chalice on his breast" (*D* 18).

The absence of Father Butler from the Pigeon House, so naively assumed by Leo Dillon, is countered with the unexpected presence of a "queer old josser" (*D* 26), who represents to the boy the "unfolding" of "some elaborate mystery" (*D* 27), just as Father Flynn had demonstrated "how complex and mysterious were certain institutions of the Church" (*D* 13). In lieu of understanding the josser's "mystery," the boy is frightened and quickly resorts to the ruse of calling Mahony to him by the prearranged pseudonym, Murphy. (But Mahony does not respond to the name—no Murphy actually exists.) The unexpected stranger in "An Encounter" is replicated throughout the volume: the arrival of the Englishman Routh disconcerts Jimmy Doyle and leads to his severe gambling losses; the unwelcome English artiste Weathers defeats Farrington at arm wrestling; the "next-door girl" is responsible for the trick played on Maria; Father Keon makes his mysterious appearance in the committee room ("I thought he was a dozen of stout," comments Mr. Henchy with regret [*D* 127]). Fogarty turns up uninvited at Kernan's bedside with a bottle of spirits, but Kernan cannot partake of the whiskey; and Bartell D'Arcy obviously is a new guest at the Morkans' party, and does not understand the traditional ceremony ("but one of his neighbours nudged him and whispered something to him upon which he allowed his glass to be filled" [*D* 201]).

It is the existence of a Michael Furey that comes as the major surprise in "The Dead"—a surprise for Gabriel Conroy, who apparently never in ten years of marriage heard his wife mention her former lover, yet it is this ghostly presence that informs the story, just as the shade of Charles Stewart Parnell, also eleven years dead, hovers over "Ivy Day in the Committee Room." [He is particularly invoked by Joe Hynes, an intrusive presence since it is assumed that he is "a man from the other camp. He's a spy of Colgan's if you ask me," declares Henchy] (*D* 124). Crofton is also an intrusive element: "He had been a canvasser for Wilkins, the Conservative, but when the Conservatives had withdrawn their man and, choosing the

lesser of two evils, given their support to the Nationalist
candidate, he had been engaged to work for Mr Tierney" (*D*
130). The juxtaposition of these two intruders from opposite
camps reaches its culmination when Hynes reads his pathetic
eulogy for the dead Parnell, and Crofton is called upon to
comment on a poem to a politician with whom he had no
sympathy; his comment is as gnomonic as it is disingenuously
elliptical: "Mr Crofton said that it was a very fine piece of
writing" (*D* 135).

For James Duffy ghosts had no significant existence: "He
lived at a little distance from his body" and "had neither
companions nor friends, church nor creed. He lived his
spiritual life without any communion with others, visiting his
relatives at Christmas and escorting them to the cemetery
when they died" (*D* 108, 109). He seems safe from the
intrusive shadows that loom across so many of the other
Dubliners, and when he finds that his presumably platonic
relationship with Mrs. Sinico evolves into uncomfortably
emotional dimensions on her part, he neatly severs his
connection with her. With a life that casts no shadow and on
which no shadow is ever allowed to fall, Duffy seems immune
by having chosen a self-inflicted paralysis of carefully limited
existence. Yet, when he reads of Mrs. Sinico's unsavory death,
he cannot for long sustain his relief in "approving of the course
he had taken" in turning away from her completely: the
shadows that now darken his mind are numerous and
complex:

he realised that she was dead, that she had died, ceased to exist, that
she had become a memory. He began to feel ill at ease. . . . His life
would be lonely too until he, too, died, ceased to exist, became a
memory— if anyone remembered him. (*D* 116)

Duffy discovers that even a ghost can be a comforting
presence, and that rather than be haunted now by the specter
of the dead Emily Sinico, as he had at first expected ("he
seemed to feel her voice touch his ear, her hand touch his"),

there was only the *absence* of a ghost to haunt him: "He could not feel her near him in the darkness nor hear her voice touch his ear. . . . He felt that he was alone" (*D* 117).

In the world of Joyce's *Dubliners*, important plum cakes get left behind on trams and corkscrews cannot be located; anticipated bazaars prove darkened and empty; dust covers the furniture although the room is regularly dusted; poems remain unread by would-be poets and documents uncopied by clerks commissioned to copy them; political canvassers go unpaid, although the eventual appearance of a "dozen of stout" soon makes them forget the missing payment; musical accompanists go unpaid, although when half of the promised four guineas is finally offered, the payment is "four shillings short" (*D* 146), and the accompanist is removed by her mother although the concert is only half over. Mrs. Kearney has brought her husband to help her negotiate the terms of her daughter's payment, but he proves inefficient, almost as if he were not present. At a religious retreat the pews are filled with politicians and pawnbrokers and moneylenders, and "poor O'Carroll, an old friend of Mr Kernan's, who had been at one time a considerable commercial figure" (*D* 172-73). At the firm of Crosbie and Alleyne, one of the partners "had hounded little Peake out of the office in order to make room for his own nephew" (*D* 92), so one may wonder what job security exists for "Little Chandler." It is a world of absence and loss, smaller portions and smaller dividends, of interposing shadows and hollow substances, constricted by paralysis, shot through with simoniac practices, and gutted by gnomonic removals.

3

The Book of Himself

Tentative Steps

Almost all of the stories contained in *Dubliners* were written
by the time James Joyce was twenty-three years old, and "The
Dead" added when he was in his twenty-fifth year. The novella
coda was the result of a bout of rheumatic fever at a crucial
point in his life, and the decision to scrap the thousand or so
manuscript pages of *Stephen Hero*, his first attempt at writing
a novel, and begin again on the quasi-autobiographical novel
was made at the same time. *Stephen Hero* looked inward into
a life, charting it meticulously and completely, and the titular
hero, Stephen Daedalus, was to be viewed by a literary process
that moved from first-person singular to the third, as in the
ballad of "Turpin Hero." In the revised *Portrait of the Artist as
a Young Man* Stephen explains his aesthetics by stating that

The simplest epical form is seen emerging out of lyrical literature
when the artist prolongs and broods upon himself as the centre of an
epical event and this form progresses till the centre of emotional
gravity is equidistant from the artist himself and from others. The
narrative is no longer purely personal. The personality of the artist

49

passes into the narration itself, flowing round and round the persons and the action like a vital sea. This progress you will see easily in that old English ballad *Turpin Hero* which begins in the first person and ends in the third person. (*AP* 214-15)

During the preceding years Joyce had worked simultaneously on the personal narrative of the artist himself and on the book of the "Others," those Dubliners who gravitated in concentric circles around the consciousness of the artist. *Dubliners* and *A Portrait* are best read as superimposed upon each other, as facing narratives of the two facets of the artist's consciousness of "Self" and "Others." The boy in the opening triad of stories comes close to the Stephen of the first chapter of *A Portrait*, sensitive and aware, observing without revealing his thoughts. At the Christmas dinner which is the centerpiece of that first chapter, Stephen registers the impact of the disruptive quarrel but is stunned into silence, much like the boy listening to the two sisters gossip about the dead priest. A sensitivity to words is also characteristic of Stephen Dedalus (Joyce had momentarily toyed with demythologizing Daedalus to a simply Daly, but settled for dropping the digraph—he saved Daly as one of the aliases used by the Dedaluses in chapter 5 when pawning their possessions), as he considers homonyms ("That was a belt round his pocket. And belt was also to give a fellow a belt" [*AP* 9]), and onomatopoeia ("Suck was a queer word. . . . Once he had washed his hands in the lavatory of the Wicklow Hotel and his father pulled the stopper up by the chain after and the dirty water went down through the hole in the basin. And when it had all gone down slowly the hole in the basin had made a sound like that: suck" [*AP* 11]), and names ("God was God's name just as his name was Stephen. *Dieu* was the French for God" [*AP* 16]). The direction of young Stephen toward the vocation of the literary artist determines the structure of *A Portrait of the Artist as a Young Man*.

Stephen Hero had the potential shape and girth of a nineteenth-century novel; *A Portrait*, afflicted with the style of scrupulous meanness Joyce had employed in *Dubliners,* points toward the modernism of the twentieth. The extant pages from the earlier version (published after Joyce's death) contain fully developed incidents, some eliminated, some retained, others merely suggested in the succeeding *Portrait,* and the economy practiced by Joyce in his revision becomes all the more apparent in contrast to the remnants of *Stephen Hero.* As soon as he began the reconstitution of his material, Joyce envisioned a book in five long chapters, the first three of which he completed within a year. The rhythmic rise and fall within each of the five parts tightens the structure of *A Portrait of the Artist as a Young Man,* as Stephen undergoes the traumatic instances of development and maturation between the infancy with which the book begins and the suspended conclusion at which the university graduate prepares to embark for Paris. Chapter 1 concludes with schoolboy Stephen in triumph, lauded by his schoolmates for having bravely defied authority by having sought redress from the rector when he had been unjustly punished by Father Dolan. Chapter 2 ends with the adolescent swooning in the arms of a prostitute for the first time, while chapter 3 ends with his return to piety, having confessed his sins and been absolved. At the end of chapter 4 the potential artist undergoes an equally spiritual conversion, having encountered his muse and embraced his vocation, rejecting the possibility of the priesthood, and at the conclusion of chapter 5 he sets out for his new career and a new life: "Welcome, O life! I go to encounter for the millionth time the reality of experience and to forge in the smithy of my soul the uncreated conscience of my race" (*AP* 252-53).

The heightened curve of Stephen's emotions are inevitably countered by the realities of his youthful experience, and each new chapter begins in sharp contrast to the exultations with which the previous one concludes. At the beginning of the second chapter Stephen is very much at loose ends: he has been withdrawn from the prestigious Jesuit boarding school because of the decline of his father's financial condition. As the third chapter opens ("The swift December dusk had come

tumbling clownishly after its dull day and, as he stared through
the dull square of the window of the schoolroom, he felt his
belly crave for its food" [*AP* 102]), the ecstasy of sexual
initiation has become a sordid commonplace, quickly
developing into morbid guilt, and although his spiritual
cleansing evokes "Another life! A life of grace and virtue and
happiness!" (*AP* 146), that life as seen at the start of the fourth
chapter is jejune, mechanical, and without spiritual enthusiasm: "Sunday was dedicated to the mystery of the Holy
Trinity, Monday to the Holy Ghost, Tuesday to the Guardian
Angels, Wednesday to Saint Joseph, Thursday to the Most
Blessed Sacrament of the Altar, Friday to the Suffering Jesus,
Saturday to the Blessed Virgin Mary" (*AP* 147). And although
the élan of his decision to become an artist is expected to carry
over through the entire last chapter, that chapter nonetheless
commences in the most banal circumstances, as Stephen drags
out his pathetic breakfast before going off late to his university
classes, as his mother scrubs his dirty neck, resentful that he
chose the university in lieu of the seminary, and his father
gratuitously curses him. The aftermath of elation is invariably
depression, and the triumph with which *A Portrait* concludes
is undercut by the deflated opening of *Ulysses*.

The Five Ages of Youth

The first chapter of *A Portrait* is particularly tight in its
patterning: the first few paragraphs deal with infancy and
preschool childhood, almost in the language and linguistic
intimations of the child, as it awakens to the reality of its
tangible senses (auditory, "His father told him that story";
visual, "he had a hairy face"; gustatory, "she sold lemon platt";
tactile, "When you wet the bed first it is warm then it gets
cold"; and olfactory, "His mother had a nicer smell than his
father" [*AP* 7]). It introduces the dramatis personae of the
child's world, parents and residing relatives, and then opens
outward to the neighboring world: "The Vances lived in
number seven. They had a different father and mother. They
were Eileen's father and mother" (*AP* 8). The pleasures and

confusions, aspirations and tensions of childhood are outlined
with concision, as the initiate threads his way through the new
experiences, culminating with an unexplained (censored)
transgression for which Stephen is threatened with
punishment. The embryonic artist listens to stories and songs,
attempts to replicate the song and dance to the music, and
when in danger of parental retribution, he combines his
mother's attempt to spare him ("Stephen will apologise")
with Dante Riordan's severity ("if not, the eagle will come and
pull out his eyes") into a piece of rhymed doggerel that
constantly repeats the opposed tensions:

> *Pull out his eyes,*
> *Apologise,*
> *Apologise,*
> *Pull out his eyes.*

> *Apologise,*
> *Pull out his eyes,*
> *Pull out his eyes,*
> *Apologise. (AP 8)*

The chiasmic juxtapositions, the natural rhymes derived from
the accidents of speech, the sustained repetitions, the
alliteration of the consonants and the diverse range of the
vowels, all attest to an instinctual poeticization of Stephen's
experience, assuaging the impact of his fear and guilt.

These paragraphs not only establish Stephen Dedalus's
artistic tendencies as well as certain leitmotifs, but also serve as
a brief overture to a chapter that is structured in sonata-allegro
form: his life at Clongowes Wood College before and then
after a Christmas vacation back at home with his parents and
uncle, Dante, and Mr. Casey. The short inner section has a
rhythm of its own, running counter to the pattern of the
chapters themselves: from the sedate introduction, "A great
fire, banked high and red, flamed in the grate and under the
ivytwined branches of the chandelier the Christmas table was
spread" (*AP* 27), to the tumultuous conclusion, the vicious

political squabble that ruins the tranquility of the holiday celebration: "Stephen, raising his terrorstricken face, saw that his father's eyes were full of tears" (*AP* 39). The equilibrium of Stephen's world, where adult authority was consistent and unified, is permanently shattered by the argument over Parnell and the Church, and conditions that prevailed for him at Clongowes prior to the Christmas dinner are no longer operative for him afterward. When he first arrived at school he bore his father's interdict in mind, "whatever he did, never to peach on a fellow" (*AP* 9), and so when he becomes sick as a result of having been pushed into the ditch by a fellow student, he is implored to remain true to the code:

A voice at his bed said:
   —Dedalus, don't spy on us, sure you won't?
   Wells's face was there. He looked at it and saw that Wells was afraid.
   —I didn't mean to. Sure you won't?
   His father had told him, whatever he did, never to peach on a fellow. He shook his head and answered no and felt glad. (*AP* 21)

The exact repetition of his father's words in Stephen's mind proves just how codified the strictures were for him, and he identifies in Wells's fears a reflection of his own when he transgressed against Eileen Vance. (In *Stephen Hero* Wells emerges as a pimple-faced seminary student, a factor that Joyce does not retain in *A Portrait;* he had used the instance of an inappropriate vocation for Joe Dillon in "An Encounter.")

Reared in an Irish Catholic family with nationalist sympathies, Stephen accepts that unity and harmony that is emblemized in Dante's two brushes ("The brush with the maroon velvet back was for Michael Davitt and the brush with the green velvet back was for Parnell"—*AP* 7), yet the dissension that set in with the disgrace of Parnell was already known to Stephen before he first went to Clongowes: "Dante had ripped the green velvet back off the brush that was for Parnell one day with her scissors and told him that Parnell was a bad man. That was called politics. There were two sides in it: Dante was on one side and his father and Mr Casey were on the other side" (*AP* 16). Nonetheless, he is relatively unfazed by the division, seeing it in the same terms as the "sides" in the classroom, as the two teams attempted to solve mathematical problems. So even when in his illness he learns of the death of Parnell, Stephen retains an image of unity: "And he saw Dante in a maroon velvet dress and with a green velvet mantle hanging from her shoulders walking proudly and silently past the people who knelt by the waters' edge" (*AP* 27).

The extreme of Dante's virulence and the sight of his father in tears at the Christmas dinner table served to derange Stephen's long-standing equilibrium. The child whose "eyes were weak and watery" (*AP* 8) kept faith with Wells the bully in conjunction with his authoritative father's command, but the Simon Dedalus whose "eyes were full of tears" is no longer the figure of authority, and during the term following the Christmas vacation Stephen finds himself in a dilemma. Falsely accused by the prefect of study as idling, he is punished although he has accidentally broken his glasses when run into on the cinder path, and considers reporting Father Dolan to the rector—in effect, peaching on a fellow, and on a priest at that. Punishment was rampant at Clongowes at the time, as several of the older boys were about to be flogged for "smugging," and little Stephen is egged on by the others to go to Father Conmee. "The fellows had told him to go but they would not go themselves," Stephen realizes. "They had forgotten all about it. No, it was best to forget all about it and perhaps the prefect of studies had only said he would come in. No, it was best to hide out of the way because when you were small and young you could often escape that way" (*AP* 54-55). Despite this "political" awareness, Stephen makes the trek to the rector's office, receives his vindication ("—Very well, the rector said, it is a mistake and I shall speak to Father Dolan myself" [*AP* 57]), and is hailed by his fellow students. Whereas the first Clongowes scene began on the playing field, where the "evening air was pale and chilly" and Stephen "kept on the fringe of the line ... feigning to run now and then" (*AP* 8), the second scene ends on the playing field, where "the air was soft and grey and mild" and Stephen listens contentedly to the sound of the cricket balls in "the soft grey silence" (*AP* 59).

The second chapter of *A Portrait* has none of the balanced structure of the first. Instead, a series of five segments of varying proportions carry the young adolescent through a handful of years, with no clear transitions between segments and diverse elements within each. The air of indeterminacy corresponds to Stephen's condition: for a while he is out of school, living in a still decent Dublin suburb; then he is a day student at Belvedere College, the family having moved into a north Dublin tenement; the childhood flirtations with Eileen are replaced with adolescent interest in Emma; from a still insecure student accused of writing heresy in a class paper and taunted by bullies for his admiration of Lord Byron, Stephen evolves into a prominent school leader, and wins essay prizes with cash awards; and he accompanies his father to Cork, where the last of the family property is sold off. Even the relationship with Emma, which seems very much at the center of Stephen's consciousness for a while during this period of his life, fades away as he makes his calculated move toward the area of prostitution and into the arms of the prostitute with "frank uplifted eyes" (*AP* 101). The chapter had begun with Stephen fantasizing on the Mercedes of *The Count of Monte Cristo,* imagining in the Blackrock suburb the "sunny trellisses" of Marseilles (*AP* 63) and centered on the Emma for whom he wrote Byronic love poetry, but who shyly escaped his grasp; it ends with an ironic recollection ("the image of Mercedes traversed the background of his memory. He saw again the small white house and the garden of rosebushes on the road that led to the mountains" [*AP* 99]), since Stephen now wanders "the dark slimy streets peering into the gloom of lanes and doorways, listening eagerly for any sound" (*AP* 99), where he surrenders to embraces of the prostitute, to "the dark pressure of her softly parting lips" (*AP* 101).

Not only do the quick transitions mirror the transitory nature of Stephen's youthful experiences, but the constant

replacement of secondary characters, people with whom
Stephen comes in contact for brief periods, establishes a
pattern that persists throughout the novel, which is quite
specifically "a portrait" of an individual character, all others
remaining incidental. Belvedere pupils and teachers replace
Clongowes pupils and teachers; Mr. and Mrs. Dedalus make
their transposition into chapter 2, and Stephen's younger
brother Maurice appears; Dante Riordan has disappeared
(presumably because of the Christmas incident), and Uncle
Charles is aging and also soon disappears; Emma (E. C.)
supplants Eileen, and several relatives make their vague
appearance temporarily. The vestiges of the childhood of the
opening chapter are viewed through Stephen's recollections:
"he remembered the day when he and Eileen stood looking
into the hotel grounds" (*AP* 69);

he had covered the page with the names and addresses of certain of
his classmates:

> Roderick Kickham
> John Lawton
> Anthony MacSwiney
> Simon Moonan (*AP* 70)

—just as his father in Cork conjures up the names of the school
fellows from his own past. But the childhood past more
seriously infringes on the adolescent present when Mr.
Dedalus announces that "the rector, or provincial, rather, was
telling me that story about you and Father Dolan," reporting
Father Conmee as saying, *"I told them all at dinner about it and
Father Dolan and I and all of us we had a hearty laugh together
over it"* (*AP* 72). Mr. Dedalus lauds the Jesuits for diplomacy,
but the effect of this casual betrayal on Stephen's consciousness
is potent yet never quite revealed.

The central chapter of *A Portrait* is quite classically
proportioned as a triptych. The short introductory panel
effects the transition from Stephen as denizen of the red-light
district to Stephen as schoolboy at Belvedere College, where a
retreat in honor of Saint Francis Xavier is announced by

Father Arnall. The extent of Stephen's guilt has not as yet been measured, but he reacts to the priest's "dark stern eyes" in anticipation of the impact of the retreat on his conscience: "In the silence their dark fire kindled the dusk into a tawny glow. Stephen's heart had withered up like a flower of the desert that feels the simoom coming from afar" (*AP* 108). The long central portion unfolds the series of hellfire sermons delivered at the retreat by Father Arnall, sermons relentless in their imprecations for sinners. It is the longest single sustained section of the book, a text that almost suspends the narrative for the constant iteration leading to the "frightful torment to those damned souls, tempters and tempted alike, of the company of the devils" (*AP* 123). The sermons build in momentum, day after day, and Stephen's reactions develop in relation to them, until "His flesh shrank together as it felt the approach of the ravenous tongues of flame, dried up as it felt about it the swirl of stifling air. . . . A wave of fire swept through his body: the first. Again a wave. His brain began to glow. Another. His brain was simmering and bubbling within the crackling tenement of the skull" (*AP* 125). Stephen's personal torment is ironically countered by the casual acceptance of the sermon by the others ("He put us all into a blue funk," comments one auditor [*AP* 125]), but for him the effect was to bring him to the act of contrition, "praying with his heart" (*AP* 135).

The brief concluding panel enlarges on the anguish suffered by Stephen on the basis of that glimpse of damnation, as he examines his licentious behavior: "The leprous company of his sins closed about him, breathing upon him, bending over him from all sides" (*AP* 137). To augment his waking torment, his dream (paralleling the dream of the dead Parnell that he had in the Clongowes infirmary) magnifies into enormous proportions the expanse of his guilt and results in a fit of vomiting:

Goatish creatures with human faces, hornybrowed, lightly bearded and grey as indiarubber. The malice of evil glittered in their hard eyes,

as they moved hither and thither, trailing their long tails behind
them. A rictus of cruel malignity lit up greyly their old bony faces.…
They moved in slow circles, circling closer and closer to enclose, to
enclose, soft language issuing from their lips, their long swishing tails
besmeared with stale shite, thrusting upwards their terrific faces. (*AP*
137-38)

In seeking a chapel in which to confess Stephen wanders far
afield from where he lives, and the old Capuchin who grants
him absolution balances in this segment of the chapter the
Father Arnall who introduces the subject of the retreat in the
first segment—although he is basically refined out of existence
in the central section by the text of the sermon itself. The
return to school where he takes communion marks for
Stephen the end of his life as a libertine and the commencement
of his life as a penitent: "The ciborium had come to him" (*AP*
146).

   The major force of each chapter is subtly undercut in each
succeeding chapter, as a series of supple links are formed to
weave the five stages of Stephen's development together. Just
as the cabal of Fathers Conmee and Dolan undermines
Stephen's triumph, so Mr. Tate, the English master at
Belvedere, plays a dual role: in chapter 2 he had accused
Stephen of heresay and consequently brought down the wrath
of the bullying Heron (an extension of the Wells of the first
chapter) on Stephen; in chapter 3 he and Heron blithely
discuss the weather and a bicycle trip, just as Stephen emerges
from the horrors of the sermon on hell. Chapter 4 brings
Stephen within reach of a clerical vocation, and his interview
with the director of studies at Belvedere parallels his interview
with Father Conmee at Clongowes. The specter of "The
Reverend Stephen Dedalus, S. J." (*AP* 161) is invoked here,
rather than that of Father Dolan, and Stephen has been
summoned rather than allowed to intrude himself into the
study of the authority figure. The temptation for Stephen is
obvious when the director suggests the possibility of a calling
("He would know then what was the sin of Simon Magus and
what the sin against the Holy Ghost for which there was no

forgiveness" [*AP* 159]), but he as quickly rejects the temptation: "He would never swing the thurible before the tabernacle as priest. His destiny was to be elusive of social or religious orders" (*AP* 162). The momentum with which he makes the negative choice might well derive from the similarity of the two interviews. At the earlier one Stephen could not help noticing that "There was a skull on the desk and a strange solemn smell in the room," and "he looked at the skull and at the rector's kindlooking face" (*AP* 56). The *momento mori* has its logical place on the priest's desk, yet Stephen might later have changed his view of Father Conmee's kindness in the light of his father's anecdote. At the second interview, therefore, he is quick to see the skull beneath the skin, to envision the death's-head as betrayal:

The director stood in the embrasure of the window, his back to the light, leaning an elbow on the brown crossblind and, as he spoke and smiled, slowly dangling and looping the cord of the other blind. Stephen stood before him, following for a moment with his eyes the waning of the long summer daylight above the roofs or the slow deft movements of the priestly fingers. The priest's face was in total shadow but the waning daylight from behind him touched the deeply grooved temples and the curves of the skull. (*AP* 153-54)

As Stephen walks out of the director's office, shaking off the idea of the priesthood for himself, the "strange solemn smell" of Conmee's office translates itself subtly as the "troubling odour of the long corridors of Clongowes came back to him" (*AP* 160).

The fourth chapter is neatly balanced into three equal parts, leading from the piety that induces the director to suggest the priesthood to Stephen to the discovery of the vocation of the artist. The monotony of religion makes itself obvious in the first part, so much so that the more Stephen indulges himself in pious acts the less the sincerity and depth of piety seem to remain, and the concluding comment ("—I have amended my life, have I not? he asked himself" [*AP* 153]) is so halfhearted as to be worthless. In the second part the director, after keeping Stephen waiting and further delaying him by his elliptical approach to the subject, further draws out the monotony, so that Stephen has essentially come to his negative decision even before the offer is made, and his journey home leads past "the faded blue shrine of the Blessed Virgin which stood fowlwise on a pole in the middle of a hamshaped encampment of poor cottages" (*AP* 162). The "fading" reflects the loss of enthusiasm of the Stephen who at Belvedere is "the prefect of Our Blessed Lady's sodality" (*AP* 157), and the home he returns to is even further depressed economically, his parents away looking for new lodgings. In the third part Stephen has elected to enter the university, and as he meanders toward North Bull Island, he encounters, much to his annoyance, a "squad of christian brothers ... on its way back from the Bull" (*AP* 165). School fellows are swimming in the river and call to him, but he avoids them as well. Instead he finds himself entranced by a wading girl, "a strange and beautiful seabird" (*AP* 171), and he translates his experience into a realization of his destiny: "His soul was swooning into some new world, fantastic, dim, uncertain as under sea, traversed by cloudy shapes and beings" (*AP* 172). From the provocative Eileen to the idealized Mercedes to the flirtatious Emma to devotion to the Blessed Virgin the rise and fall of Stephen's erotic-religious ecstasies culminate in the birdgirl on the strand: "—Heavenly God! cried Stephen's soul, in an outburst of profane joy" (*AP* 171).

Chapter 5 is disproportionately far more extensive than any of the previous four, a bringing together of all the threads spun through the expanding text. Three major sections are followed by a short coda that alters the style and narrational strategy, and each of the long portions maintains a complex sweep and flow of narrative events. The opening in the Dedalus home completes the series of glimpses into the financial decline of the family tracked through each of the chapters, to which has been added the burgeoning number of Stephen's siblings. The descent from the Christmas feast of turkey and ham and celery and plum pudding now seems complete as Stephen drains "his third cup of watery tea to the dregs" and chews "the crusts of fried bread" (*AP* 174). Stephen's escape from this pathetic dwelling takes him past "the nuns' madhouse," where a mad nun is screeching, "Jesus! O Jesus! Jesus!" (*AP* 175), and he makes his way to the university through the northeast quadrant of Dublin, transforming each feature of the prosaic cityscape into rememberd experiences from literature— Hauptmann, Newman, Cavalcanti, Ibsen, Ben Jonson. Traversing Dublin at this stage of his life duplicates his first wanderings as an adolescent when the Dedaluses moved from the suburbs into the city ("Dublin was a new and complex sensation" to him then as he encountered the "vastness and strangeness of the life suggested to him by the bales of merchandise stocked along the walls" of the Dublin docks [*AP* 66])—even then he had tried to reconcile reality with the life of the imagination, superimposing the Marseilles of Alexandre Dumas on his own Dublin. (Later, in *Ulysses* Stephen reflects, "Dublin. I have much, much to learn" [*U* 144].)

The bulk of the first section depicts Stephen at the National University and environs, as does the third section, the two flanking the middle section of Stephen at home in bed, so that chapter 5 is an enlarged mirror image of chapter 1—the coda portion balancing the childhood portion. The university scenes are a series of confrontations for Stephen, mostly with fellow students who as representatives of their society make certain demands of him and challenge him into open opposition. These students, especially Cranly, Lynch, Davin, and MacCann, are better developed characterizations than any previously created in *A Portrait,* as if they depict counter-portraits for Stephen Dedalus. The change from the fourth to the fifth chapter marks the transition for Stephen into young manhood, and the narrative that now contains him no longer uses the protective language that reflects primarily the inner Stephen, his perspective cloaked in deceptively objective narration. Whereas at the end of the previous chapter he had anticipated the university with eager excitement ("The university! So he had passed beyond the challenge of the sentries who had stood as guardians of his boyhood and had sought to keep him among them that he might be subject to them and serve their ends" [*AP* 165]), Stephen now has no illusions about the university, and it is apparent from his conversation with the dean of studies there that he already feels intellectually superior to his intended mentors. With his associates he develops an aloofness that at times amounts to arrogance, and he recalls MacCann admonishing him as "an antisocial being, wrapped up in yourself" (*AP* 177). From his own perspective and in his own defense he announces to Cranly, "I will try to express myself in some mode of life or art as freely as I can and as wholly as I can, using for my defence the only arms I allow myself to use—silence, exile, and cunning" (*AP* 247).

As a Belvedere schoolboy Stephen had been implicitly aware of the claims upon him by the various authorities of the adult world:

he had heard about him the constant voices of his father and of his masters, urging him to be a gentleman above all things and urging him to be a good catholic above all things. These voices had now come to be hollowsounding in his ears. When the gymnasium had been opened he had heard another voice urging him to be strong and manly and healthy and when the movement towards national revival had begun to be felt in the college yet another voice had bidden him be true to his country and help to raise up her fallen language and tradition. In the profane world, as he foresaw, a worldly voice would bid him raise up his father's fallen state by his labours and, meanwhile, the voice of his school comrades urged him to be a decent fellow, to shield others from blame or to beg them off and to do his best to get free days for the school. (*AP* 83-84)

Sophisticated versions of these voices still prove operative in Stephen's university days, especially tempting when they come close to ideals he found appealing and compromises that he might find convenient. In the first instance MacCann and Davin sought his participation in international and nationalist causes; in the second Lynch and Cranly presented themselves as friends and tried to lessen the severity of Stephen's withdrawal, suggesting self-interest and reminding him of the comforts of the Church.

During the long walk to the University, Stephen listens in retrospect to the voices of Davin and MacCann (throughout *A Portrait* he is constantly "receiving" messages, such as those that insist that he apologize and that he never peach on a fellow). Stephen by now has established himself as a formidable presence, and MacCann for one cannot quite urge and insist as others have before him. Instead he differentiates between himself and Stephen, whom he brands as antisocial, insisting that he himself is a "democrat" working "for social liberty and equality among all classes and sexes in the United States of the Europe of the future" (*AP* 177). The high-sounding claim is not the sort that Stephen can summarily dismiss, but when he meets MacCann at the University soliciting signatures for the Russian Czar's peace petition, Stephen can express his disdain for the image of the Czar, calling into question the legitimacy of the campaign. MacCann reacts to Stephen's insistence that "You are right to go your way. Leave me to go mine" by saying, "Dedalus . . . I believe you're a good fellow but you have yet to learn the dignity of altruism and the responsibility of the human individual" (*AP* 198-99), which will have a strange reechoing at the end of *A Portrait,* Stephen recalling his mother's words: "She prays now, she says, that I may learn in my own life and away from home and friends what the heart is and what it feels" (*AP* 252).

Davin's appeal is far more personal, and Stephen is hardly as brutal in demolishing his nationalistic arguments as the Stephen of *Stephen Hero* had been with his predecessor. He is the only friend who calls him "Stevie," and although he considers Davin a "peasant student" with a "rude Firbolg mind" and calls him "one of the tame geese" (*AP* 180-81), Stephen reveals in his estimation of him an urban dweller's terror of the mysteries of the remote countryside. What he remembers about Davin in particular is an incident he had related about being invited in by a partially dressed young

peasant woman in the doorway of a lonely country cottage late
at night, an invitation from which Davin had fled, but which
Stephen's imagination translates into more extensive
perspectives. He remembers again his Clongowes days and
superimposes Davin's experience upon his own observations:

The last words of Davin's story sang in his memory and the figure of
the woman in the story stood forth, reflected in other figures of the
peasant women whom he had seen standing in the doorways at Clane
as the college cars drove by, as a type of her race and his own, a batlike
soul waking to the consciousness of itself in darkness and secrecy and
loneliness and, through the eyes and voice and gesture of a woman
without guile, calling the stranger to her bed. (*AP* 183)

In his quest for the womanly ideal that he associates with the
soul of Ireland, Stephen later attaches to Emma the same
attributes of the peasant woman: "she was a figure of the
womanhood of her country," he says of Emma, "a batlike soul
waking to the consciousness of itself in darkness and secrecy
and loneliness, tarrying awhile, loveless and sinless" (*AP* 221).
Davin's hardheaded political militancy, however, fails to find a
response in Stephen's imagination, and although the young
enthusiast insists that "a man's country comes first. Ireland
first, Stevie," Stephen rejects the idea out of hand, commenting
caustically that "Ireland is the old sow that eats her farrow"
(*AP* 203).

   Lynch and Cranly somehow manage to come closer in under
Stephen's guard, establishing claims of personal friendship
that he later assumes they have betrayed (Cranly by the end of
A Portrait and Lynch toward the end of *Ulysses*). It is to Lynch
that Stephen unfolds his theories of aesthetics, although there
is very little in Lynch's responses to indicate that he
apprehends the subtlety of Stephen's concepts. He serves as a
sounding board, goading rather than encouraging the flow of
Stephen's ideas, asserting that one of Stephen's pithy enigmas
"has the true scholastic stink" (*AP* 214); but eventually tiring
of intellectual discourse he puts an end to the conversation by
asking "surlily": "What do you mean . . . by prating about

beauty and the imagination in this miserable Godforsaken island?" (*AP* 215). Lynch's primary concern is with material needs, his poverty similar to Stephen's, from whom he cadges cigarettes as the price of his attention: "If I am to listen to your esthetic philosophy give me at least another cigarette. I don't care about it. I don't even care about women. . . . I want a job of five hundred a year. You can't get me one" (*AP* 207).

Cranly's claim is probably the most insidious as he extracts from Stephen the personal details of his life, of the quarrel with his family over his rejection of his religion. Stephen's confession provokes a constant series of catechistical inquiries: "I don't want to pry into your family affairs," he says (*AP* 241), but his constant prying reveals the full extent to which Stephen's father is a financial failure wallowing in his nostalgic self-importance; that the Dedalus family consists of "nine or ten" children ("Some died," Stephen comments [*AP* 241]); and that it is Stephen's mother who is most pained by his falling away from the Church, and the source of his major feelings of guilt. The confession also allows Stephen to issue policy statements about himself and his determination to change his life, to leave Ireland. "I will not serve that in which I no longer believe," he declares, "whether it call itself my home, my fatherland or my church." He adds, "You made me confess the fears that I have. But I will tell you also what I do not fear. I do not fear to be alone or to be spurned for another or to leave whatever I have to leave. And I am not afraid to make a mistake, even a great mistake, a lifelong mistake and perhaps as long as eternity too" (*AP* 247). Cranly is skillful in his temptations, allowing that even as a disbeliever Stephen could safely shelter within the bosom of the Church, keeping his apostasy quiet and profiting by his deception, and he offers as well his friendship, "the noblest and truest friend a man ever had" (*AP* 247).

The inner section of chapter 5 is fixed in Stephen's home, as he awakens before dawn and writes his religio-erotic "villanelle of the temptress" to Emma (and the Blessed Virgin). The bracketing of the section between vignettes of life at the university seems all the more purposeful by the use of allusions to birds both immediately before and immediately after: as Stephen and Lynch take shelter from the rain under the arcade of the National Library, Emma is seen there, and Stephen wonders, "If her life were a simple rosary of hours, her life simple and strange as a bird's life, gay in the morning, restless all day, tired at sundown" (*AP* 216); after the writing of the poem, he once again finds himself at the library steps, watching the birds fly by, wondering, "What birds were they? . . . He watched their flight; bird after bird. . . . He listened to the cries. . . . Why was he gazing upwards from the steps of the porch, hearing their shrill twofold cry, watching their flight? For an augury of good or evil?" (*AP* 224). The significance of birds for Stephen weaves its way from the punishing, eye-gouging eagle to the threatening football on the Clongowes playing field, "the greasy leather orb flew like a heavy bird through the grey light" (*AP* 8), to the hand-wounding pandybat: "Why did Mr Barrett in Clongowes call his pandybat a turkey?" (*AP* 30). The menace of the bird of prey, even in its domesticated form, reaches its culmination in Belvedere when Stephen is threatened by Vincent Heron ("He often thought it strange that Vincent Heron had a bird's face as well as a bird's name" [*AP* 76]), and beaten by him when he refuses to renounce his admiration for Byron. He survives the threat by establishing himself as a leader in the school, and Heron's later attempts to bully him are diminished into "friendly" teasing about Emma, which Stephen adroitly counters.

Like a frightened primitive Stephen has learned to metamorphose himself symbolically into the totem of his fear, and the charting of Stephen's development in *A Portrait* leads to the assumption of the guise of the hawklike man that becomes his totem. At the turning point, the trek to North Bull Island, his fellow Belvedereans playfully attempt to entice him into joining them in the water, and call to him as the sacrificial ox, "Stephanos Dedalos! Bous Stephanoumenos! Bous Stephaneforos!" (*AP* 168):

Now, at the name of the fabulous artificer, he seemed to hear the noise of dim waves and to see a winged form flying above the waves and slowly climbing the air. What did it mean? Was it a quaint device opening a page of some medieval book of prophecies and symbols, a hawklike man flying sunward above the sea, a prophecy of the end he had been born to serve and had been following through the mists of childhood and boyhood, a symbol of the artist forging anew in his workshop out of the sluggish matter of the earth a new soaring impalpable imperishable being? (*AP* 169)

The image of the wading girl follows almost immediately, as a reply to the questions posed ("She seemed like one whom magic had changed into the likeness of a strange and beautiful seabird" [*AP* 171])—the tentative "seemed" links the two experiences into a single continuous quest. Stephen is at once the rebellious, experimental, questing Icarus, doomed to death by drowning, and his father the fabulous artificer Daedalus, the forger in the workshop, and his redemption seems linked to the "birdgirl" that is his muse and madonna.

Although Stephen has argued in his expostulation with Lynch for the value of static rather than kinetic art, his villanelle is nonetheless inspired by an erotic dream: "His soul was all dewy wet. Over his limbs in sleep pale cool waves of light had passed" (*AP* 217). He sets himself the task of transforming the dream into poetic form, a villanelle that he works through with persistence, transcribing it on an empty cigarette packet. His depiction of the artistic inspiration retains its spiritual component ("In the virgin womb of the imagination the word was made flesh. Gabriel the seraph had come to the virgin's chamber" [*AP* 217]), although the sexual assumptions within that interpretation remain apparent. He manages to sustain the initial impetus through the first three stanzas of the involved verse form, but his thoughts shift to the object of his desire, the Emma whom he mistrusts as bourgeois and orthodox, so although the prosaic poverty of his own room fails to defuse his inspiration, the momentum is somewhat disturbed by his images of Emma at the Gaelic League with Father Moran, and only the remembering of common, flirtatious girls carries him through the next two stanzas. But with only the envoi left to compose, inspiration seriously flags when dawn begins to intrude, and his assumptions that Emma will show his verses to her uncle, a priest, deflate him to such an extent that only masturbation renews the kinetic impulse for the completion of the poem: "A glow of desire kindled again his soul and fired and fulfilled all his body. Conscious of his desire she was waking from odorous sleep, the temptress of his villanelle" (*AP* 223). The tension between the idealized beloved, the Virgin and birdgirl who wears the Blessed Virgin's colors ("slateblue skirts were kilted boldly about her waist and dovetailed behind her" [*AP* 171]), and the prosaic woman who flirts with priests and fails to recognize "a priest of eternal imagination" (*AP* 221) sustains itself into the closure of *A Portrait of the Artist as a Young Man*.

The closing coda radically alters the narrative discourse: diary entries replace the third-person articulation of events, so that Stephen's voice—or at least his "literary" voice—takes full command. The twenty-two entries cover almost twice as many days, are varied in length, frequency, and style, and often diverse in tone, from direct reportage ("Began with a discussion with my mother" [*AP* 248]), through the recording of a dream and the writing of poetic vignettes, to ironic commentary ("Puzzled for the moment by saint John at the Latin gate. What do I see? A decollated precursor trying to pick the lock" [*AP* 248]), effusive expostulation ("Wild spring. Scudding clouds. O life!" [*AP* 250]), and self-deflation ("O, give it up, old chap! Sleep it off!" [*AP* 252]). Many of the characters make their brief appearances: Stephen's mother and father (from the Christmas dinner on, the two are always separate entities); Davin, Lynch, and Cranly; and of course Emma, whose name has disappeared from the text since the middle of chapter 3, where Stephen had imagined their marriage conducted by the Virgin (now he thinks of her only in the anonymous third person: "Have not seen her since that night"; "She is not out yet"; "Saw her drinking tea": "Met her

today pointblank in Grafton Street" [*AP* 248, 249, 250, 252]).
New characters, however, also make their belated appearance,
so that as the culminating pages close down the events of
Stephen's early life, they also open new possibilities and new
directions. The English Jesuit dean of studies at the university
had, during his conversation with Stephen, balked at the word
"tundish"; Stephen now lays the matter to rest with brutal
finality: "I looked it up and find it English and good old blunt
English too. Damn the dean of studies and his funnel! What
did he come here for to teach us his own language or to learn it
from us? Damn him one way or the other!" (*AP* 251). Yet a
dialogue has opened up with Father Ghezzi: "This time about
Bruno the Nolan. . . . He said Bruno was a terrible heretic. I said
he was terribly burned" (*AP* 249). Davin's tales of the Irish
countryside had alerted Stephen to the dark, batlike soul of
Irish women that he interprets as the conscience of the Irish
race, but now someone named John Alphonsus Mulrennan is
recorded as having told an anecdote of an old man in the west
of Ireland, whom Stephen conceptualizes as a demonic
presence of ignorance and superstition:

I fear him. I fear his redrimmed horny eyes. It is with him I must
struggle all through this night till day come, till he or I lie dead,
gripping him by the sinewy throat till . . . Till what? Till he yield to
me? No. I mean him no harm. (*AP* 252)

    The major motif that remains constantly open and fluid in
the novel is that of the impossible ideal of beauty, elliptical and
complex, that eludes as well as entices the creative artist. Its
origin is in the introductory section and its reconstitution
(without resolution) is in the culminating coda. When the
child attempted to replicate the song about *"the wild rose
blossoms / On the little green place,"* he inadvertently changes
the terms to a *"green wothe"* (*AP* 7), and as a schoolboy he still
wonders about roses: "Lavender and cream and pink roses
were beautiful to think of. Perhaps a wild rose might be like
those colours and he remembered the song about the wild rose
blossoms on the little green place. But you could not have a

green rose. But perhaps somewhere in the world you could"
(*AP* 12). The quest for the green rose, an Irish quest that
nonetheless will send him into exile "somewhere in the
world," finds the university graduate packing his "new
secondhand clothes" (*AP* 252), as he affirms to the nationalist
Davin that "the shortest way to Tara was *via* Holyhead" (*AP*
250). He acknowledges Yeats as the Irish poet in quest of
aesthetic beauty, but insists on his own superior understanding
of the involuted nature of that quest:

Michael Robartes remembers forgotten beauty and, when his arms
wrap her round, he presses in his arms the loveliness which has long
faded from the world. Not this. Not at all. I desire to press in my arms
the loveliness which has not yet come into the world. (*AP* 251)

The Stephen Dedalus who prepares to depart is the self-
proclaimed Icarus who had announced to Davin that "When
the soul of a man is born in this country there are nets flung at
it to hold it back from flight. You talk to me of nationality,
language, religion. I shall try to fly by those nets" (*AP* 203). He
turns his back on the equivocal beloved, already believing that
Cranly has become her new admirer and, therefore, the one
who most insisted on friendship has betrayed him; he rejects
all claims on him by Ireland and the Roman Catholic Church;
and he dismisses with pain the admonitions of his mother and
with silent disdain the wishes of his father ("Wants me to read
law. Says I was cut out for that. More mud, more crocodiles"
[*AP* 250]). It was his father who told him the first story and
"looked at him through a glass: he had a hairy face" (*AP* 7), but
Stephen, who had immediately identified himself with the
central figure of the story ("He was baby tuckoo" [*AP* 7]), now
usurps his father's role as storyteller, although he retains his
privileged position at the center of his narrative, and in the
diary he finally does so in written discourse. The father he
invokes in the last entry is the fabulous forger Daedalus, rather
than the hairy-faced "storyteller" and "praiser of his own past"
(*AP* 241) that is Simon Dedalus. "Old father, old artificer," he

incants, "stand me now and ever in good stead" (*AP* 253),
returning not to the opening lines of the text but to the
epigraph that precedes it. Because it is a "Portrait of the Artist"
Joyce's novel is a book of magical transformation (and because
it is a portrait of the artist "as a Young Man" it is an open-
ended narrative without resolution), as Stephen Dedalus
undergoes the initiation into the unknown arts:

Et ignotas animum dimittit in artes.
[And sends the soul into the unknown arts.]

4

A Drama in Exile

The outbreak of the Great War in 1914 caught the Joyces in Austrian Trieste as British nationals, yet Joyce forged ahead after a lapse in completing *A Portrait* and beginning the writing of *Ulysses,* until he was allowed to leave for neutral Switzerland a year later. He interrupted the work on *Ulysses,* however, to undertake a third dramatic work—and the only one to survive—the play *Exiles.* Throughout his life thereafter Joyce hovered protectively over his one surviving play, concerned about productions, publications, and translations. On one hand it represented a relic of his probational period as a young writer searching for a medium, writing poems, plays, and stories in his late adolescence; on the other hand it exists as the mature work to which he dedicated himself between *A Portrait* and *Ulysses,* and although not exactly an "interlude" between those two masterpieces, it is a transitional work and supplements his attitude toward the status of the writer depicted in the two novels. *Exiles* interrupts the tracking of the young writer's development to project him into a future role, that of an accomplished and published author returning to Ireland from self-exile in Italy, and as such mirrors both Joyce's position in 1915 (with *Dubliners* in print and *A Portrait* in the offing) and an acting out of an imaginary role: called back to Dublin with prospects of recognition awaiting him. The writer in *Exiles* is named Richard Rowan, but vestiges of Stephen Dedalus still adhere to him.

Joyce's youthful enthusiasm for Henrik Ibsen, for what he oddly called Ibsen's "wayward boyish spirit," may still cling to *Exiles,* and the play certainly is in the way of Joyce's homage to the old master of the modern spirit in drama. Like many an Ibsen play (*Hedda Gabler,* for example) *Exiles* begins with the homecoming of the main character: Rowan arrives back in Ireland after nine years in Rome, bringing back the woman who had gone into exile with him, but with whom he remains unmarried, and their eight-year-old son. The death of Rowan's mother, and the consequent inheritance from his father's will, has brought him home, to a residence in suburban Merrion—a far cry from the seedy dwellings inhabited by Stephen Dedalus. He picks up just about where he had left off nine years earlier, with his journalist friend Robert Hand as a neighbor, and Hand's cousin and former fiancée Beatrice Justice giving piano lessons to young Archie Rowan. The past is in the process of being recaptured, but the major change in Rowan's status is that he is a published writer for whom Hand is attempting to arrange a position at the university. Knowing what we know about Joyce at this point in his life, Rowan's new advantages are within the realm of wish fulfillment for the poverty-stricken exile unhonored in his native land. Rowan is blessed with a paternal inheritance and a villa, a house servant, and a triumphal reentry into Ireland, with a potential for being honored and rewarded there. With all friends as prospective betrayers, however, and all women as possible sources of literary inspiration, the stage is set for the acting out of various inevitabilities.

Thematically *Exiles* reveals itself to be within the Joycean mainstream, and its directness as dramatic statement and presentation clarifies various positions taken by Joyce during the early stages of his literary career. A concern with betrayal in multiple ways pervades the play: personal and political, sexual and spiritual, collective and individual. At the center of the complex web is Richard Rowan himself, although by no means the only victim of betrayals, often the betrayer as well, but always at the center of the web. His role in relation to Ireland provides only a minor thread, interlaced with many others: that he went into self-imposed exile from Ireland with Bertha has been considered a betrayal of nation, as well as a defiance of the moral strictures of that nation, so that his return is ambiguously perceived. The belated inheritance gives him a foothold (in the fashionable outskirts of Dublin City), and the offer of a chair in romance languages at the university would give him an entrenched position. Hand's campaign on its behalf is heralded in the first act when Richard is informed of an invitation to dine with the vice-chancellor, and reiterated in the last act: Hand has published a leading article called *"A Distinguished Irishman"* (*E* 128).

Robert's motives prove suspect, as he admits in the second act, when Richard confronts him regarding his attentions toward Bertha. His interest in arranging a permanent place for his friend includes assuring Bertha's presence as well. He nervously proposes the dinner meeting at the vice-chancellor's, like a panderer arranging an assignation, and Richard, fully aware of Robert's approaches to Bertha, adds to his nervousness by his own casual indifference toward the vice-chancellor and the suggested appointment. In act 2 Richard is rather fiendish in his calculated discomfiting of Robert, arriving at the cottage where Robert is waiting for Bertha just at the hour that Robert scheduled Richard to be at the vice-chancellor's. In act 3 Richard's thrust changes to ironic hauteur. When he is given the newspaper to read about himself he coyly mistakes the intended article to be the one headed "Death of the Very Reverend Canon Mulhall," but soon manages to locate the one about himself. He reads aloud to Beatrice: "Not the least vital of the problems which confront our country is the problem of her attitude towards those of her children who, having left her in her hour of need. . . ." He does not pause at the implied criticism of his defection, but stops reading when he notices Bertha's presence. And to Beatrice's innocent statement, "You see, Mr Rowan, your day has dawned at last. Even here. And you see that you have a warm friend in Robert, a friend who understands you," he is quick to respond: "Did you notice the little phrase at the beginning: *those who left her in her hour of need?*" (*E* 129). Joyce is quite exact in his Notes to *Exiles:* "The play is three cat and mouse acts" (*E* 156).

Richard is soon able to compound the irony in his treatment of Robert Hand's valedictory leading article, sensitive to the implication also of cowardly self-aggrandizement in the continuing segment, "have been called back to her now on the eve of her longawaited victory." (Joyce began writing *Exiles* in the early days of the First World War, the event which allowed Britain to circumvent that supposed victory for nationalist Ireland, the granting of Home Rule.) The insults are enough for Richard Rowan, providing him with the ammunition he needs against Robert Hand, but also against Bertha, who may actually have betrayed him the night before with Robert in the Ranelagh cottage. "Why, then, did you leave me last night?" Bertha asks in her own defense. "In your hour of need," comments Richard in lieu of an answer (*E* 133).

The uneasy relationship that Richard feels between himself and Ireland is reflected and refracted at various instances, with those nearest to him and the larger world without. (Proximity is a disquieting factor throughout the play: the Rowan house is apparently adjoined to that of Robert Hand, who lives with his mother, separated by their respective gardens, and Beatrice lives with the Hands as well, a cousin to Robert with whom he once was in love and who still harbors uncomfortable feelings toward him.) Primarily it is as a literary artist that Richard views himself in relation to his nation, and aware of his new prestige, and as someone who—as his old servant Brigid maintains—if he "had to meet a grand highup person he'd be twice as grand himself" (*E* 117), Richard is pointedly caustic when informed that the vice-chancellor "has the highest opinion of you, Richard. He has read your book, he said."

RICHARD

Did he buy it or borrow it?

ROBERT

Bought it, I hope.

RICHARD

... Thirtyseven copies have now been sold in Dublin. (*E* 44)

Joyce's handling of ironic language is masterful here: in both Robert's "he said" and "I hope" the vice-chancellor's case is undercut, Robert the instrument of his own defeat, and Richard's hand inadvertently strengthened.

As a writer, Richard Rowan has an even more complex entanglement with those around him, particularly in his somewhat mysterious involvement with Beatrice Justice. In her noncerebral approach Bertha is exact in sensing that the "intellectual" woman has an advantage and a hold on Rowan, but Beatrice herself can neither comprehend nor respond to his interest in her. In the opening encounter she is (against her pronounced intentions) in direct contact with him, discomfited by his directness. He confronts her with her absence of twelve days, wants to know if he has acted badly toward her, implies that she is the immediate subject of his new work, and reminds her that her letters to him in Rome established a sort of bond between them. She, on the other hand, seems to admit that giving Archie piano lessons is an excuse for coming to the Rowan house, that she prefers to avoid embarrassing personal questions, and that her former love for Robert was dissipated when she compared him to Richard: "I saw in him a pale reflection of you: then that too faded" (*E* 21). The tenuous relationship between Richard and Beatrice provides the opening conflict of the drama, yet it disappears early in the first act, not to resurface again until the third, the Richard-Bertha-Robert triangle dominating in the interim.

Bertha accosts Beatrice in act 3, positioning her so that she has to admit that she was in some ways responsible for Richard's decision to return to Ireland ("By your letters to him and then by speaking to your cousin" [*E* 124]). She proves relentless in her dealing with Beatrice, finally accusing her of being "very intimate in this house" (*E* 125), but most particularly she is perceptive in intuiting the relationship between Richard as a writer and Beatrice Justice: "He passes the greater part of the night in there writing. Night after night. ... Yes. He is writing. And it must be about something which has come into his life lately—since we came back to Ireland. Some change. Do you know that any change has come into his life? [*She looks searchingly at her.*] Do you know it or feel it?" (*E* 125). Beatrice deflects the accusation with a reminder that Robert is also "intimate" in the Rowan house, but she has been observed in the first scene being made aware of her role as inspiration for Richard Rowan's art, and whereas Bertha is exact in her sense of the artist-subject inter-relationship, Beatrice is neither honest enough nor brave enough to acknowledge the bind. "If I were a painter and told you I had a book of sketches of you you would not think it so strange, would you?" (*E* 16). Beatrice insists—and Richard admits—that the case is not quite the same.

Richard Rowan claims for himself a unique privilege in this case, making demands upon the woman who serves as his inspiration, subject, muse, critic, and apparently enlarges those demands to include her as a woman—something that Beatrice is unable to accept. As such he reserves for himself dual rights, and maintains that his recompense for unusually excessive claims is the degree of freedom that he grants to Bertha in their "marriage." He took her away with him nine years before without offering her the sanctity of the marriage rite, knowing that she would have preferred such a rite and its concomitant privileges, and allowed them to live in relative poverty in Rome, rather than accept money from his disapproving mother. He was repeatedly unfaithful and confessed his guilty adventures to her, although she herself remained faithful to him. While in Rome Richard was safe in having Bertha with him and Beatrice as a constant correspondent. Now back in Ireland, both Robert and Beatrice are uncomfortably close, with just the expanse of the two gardens separating them, and Robert is in full attendance on Bertha, while Beatrice is near but "distant."

The involvement of the Irish writer both with Ireland and with his art is never far from the surface in any Joycean scenario, but the interpersonal entanglements of the people in *Exiles* dominate the play. The possibility of an evolving love triangle is apparent from the opening scene in which Beatrice proves both drawn to Richard and resolute in her resistance to him that suggests an overpowering psychological frigidity. Although she cannot help being aware of Bertha's central position in relation to Richard, she steers away from ever mentioning her, and it is only late in their conversation that Richard does so when he refers to "me" and "mine." Beatrice fails to make the necessary connection, asking, "From you and from . . . ?" so that it is Richard who asserts, "From Bertha and from me and from our child" (*E* 23-24). Richard also tends to think in terms of a very different triangle, one from the past that he is attempting to dismantle as he interrogates her on her past relationship with Robert Hand:

RICHARD

Yet that separated me from you. I was a third person, I felt. Your names were always spoken together, Robert and Beatrice, as long as I can remember. It seemed to me, to everyone. . .

BEATRICE

We were first cousins. It is not strange that we were often together.

RICHARD

He told me of your secret engagement with him. He had no secrets from me; I suppose you know that.

BEATRICE

[*Uneasily.*] What happened—between us—is so long ago. I was a child. (*E* 20)

Richard's reference to childhood revolves full circle to arrive eventually at Beatrice's insistence that she was a child, a factor of innocence (and of innocence lost) that pervades Joyce's *Exiles*.

Richard is persistent in this enforced dialogue in prizing up the rock, in bringing the past into the present, the distant into the foreground, the secret into the open, just as Beatrice is equally determined to conceal, dissipate, defuse, confine everything to sealed boxes. In the "three cat and mouse acts" Richard is the major cat, a role that he tries to monopolize throughout but may find himself relinquishing before the end. In this scene he is the "attack cat," except that the mouselike Beatrice, who confesses to a "want of courage," survives through intransigence. There is little doubt that she is fortified by her dour religion as a "black Protestant," by a confirmed virginity—of soul as well as of body—and by a brush with death that has left her "convalescent" rather than actively alive: "As I did not die then they tell me I shall probably live. I am given life and health again—when I cannot use them" (*E* 21). Against such formidable passivity Richard's constant thrusts are unrepelled yet unprevailing, and the mouse slithers away.

The triangle Richard had chosen for himself was one in which he was the only male figure (Robert presumably abandoned in the past as the cousin who faded out of contention). And as long as he and Bertha remained in Italy that triangle remained in force: he dominated Bertha soul and body, and retained access to the mind of the admiring Beatrice. Once he is back (and on several occasions it is emphasized that these past three months have been eventful for him), he has to face the spiritual and physical coldness of Beatrice's refusal to establish contact, and the emergency of a new and threatening triangle involving Robert and Bertha. Although *Exiles* begins with a feint toward the minor triangle, the drama quickly moves toward the dominance of the major triangle, the minor one nonetheless inexorably bound into the major—a four-cornered triangle. Toward the end of act 3 Robert Hand attempts to extricate himself from the configuration, twice denying his role either in the present or even in the past: "She is yours, as she was nine years ago, when you met her first." ("When we met her first," Richard insists [*E* 139]). Although Robert accepts the corrective, he is never comfortable with it and soon tries to slip back into the granting of primacy to Richard: "Bertha is yours now as she was nine years ago, when you—when we—met her first" (*E* 141). Whatever may have taken place the previous night at the Ranelagh cottage has resulted in Robert's strange abdication in the morning.

Nor are the two triangles (Richard/Bertha/Beatrice—Bertha/Richard/Robert) ever quite discrete from each other. The conflict that results between the men reaches its climax in the second act and a resolution of sorts in the third; the implied conflict between the women is precipitously brought to the surface by Bertha (Beatrice again reluctant to engage in any direct confrontation), and undergoes an important trans-formation. All conflicts between parts of this many-headed monster are operative throughout the three cat-and-mouse acts in a drama that strings together some fifteen duologues, five in act 1, three in act 2, and seven in act 3. With Archie and Brigid effecting the transitions between the scenes of hand-to-hand combat, all possible permutations of such interaction are made possible in *Exiles*.

No sooner has Beatrice extricated herself from Richard's incursions than she falls victim to the combined attentions of Robert and Bertha—probably the only instance in the play when two cats attack simultaneously. Robert is disturbed by having Beatrice witness his arrival with overblown roses for Bertha, while Bertha masks her discomfort by overzealously playing the hostess, insisting that Beatrice stay for tea. Maintaining that it is only Archie's piano lesson that brought her so unexpectedly to the Rowan house immediately upon her return from her visit to her father's house in Youghal, Beatrice is disadvantaged in not having remembered to bring the music for the lesson. Robert presses his advantage when he concludes that Beatrice's trip to Youghal was in the manner of a "retreat," where she goes "when the protestant strain in her prevails—gloom, seriousness, righteousness" (*E* 33). Beatrice effects her retreat from the overly cavalier cousin and the overly solicitous hostess by going off with Archie for a short lesson, and escaping afterwards without having to take tea at the Rowans'.

With Beatrice out of the way the primary action of *Exiles*
has a clear field. Robert as amorous pursuer baldly plays his
hand, and succeeds in embracing a presumably compliant
Bertha, but it is apparent from the beginning that she is toying
with him almost maliciously, forcing him to woo with words,
cross-examining him with literal questions, and displaying
little enthusiasm despite her compliance. The assignation set
for that evening at the cottage, Robert remains none too sure
of her intentions. "I promise nothing," says Bertha; "I will
wait," he feebly replies (*E* 43). They have been interrupted by
Richard's return, and the would-be lover finds himself having
to stay on and politely encounter the unsuspecting husband to
whom he constantly reaffirms his strong friendship. In his
guilt Robert is almost as much a wooer of Richard as he was of
Bertha, and almost as awkward. All occasions seem to inform
against him as Richard inexplicably assumes the role of the
playful cat in dealing with his friend, who has ostensibly come
to arrange Richard's meeting with the vice-chancellor, and is
immediately put on the defensive regarding that dignitary's
reading of Richard's book: "Well, the matter is closed for the
present," Robert declares; "You have your iron mask on today"
(*E* 44).

Every topic of conversation adds to Richard's easy
accumulation of subtle victories, especially Robert's unfortunate
reference to the past, the clandestine elopement of Richard
and Bertha ("How shall I put it? . . . With a girl not exactly your
equal" [*E* 45]). Robert even risks a direct assault—"It was her
own free choice, you will say. But was she really free to
choose?" (*E* 47)—which Richard quickly turns against him,
declaring himself the victor: "I played for her against all that
you say or can say; and I won" (*E* 47). The audience is acutely
aware that the subject of Bertha is the wrong one at this
moment for Robert, and he belatedly shifts to the nostalgic
past when the two men shared the Ranelagh cottage for
"Drinking and blasphemy" (Robert), "And drinking and
heresy" (Richard). Richard turns this safe area also into his
field of combat:

RICHARD
And some others.

ROBERT
[*Lightly, uneasily.*] You mean the women. I have no remorse of conscience. Maybe you have. We had two keys on those occasions. [*Maliciously.*] Have you? (*E* 48)

For Robert to admit to no remorse of conscience, to prattle on about his libertine doctrine and claim all women as his "natural" domain, is perceived as weighted with irony by an audience that knows his intentions toward Bertha, but also assumes that Richard does not.

How much more ironic then when the next scene reveals that Richard has known of the approaches from the very first, that Bertha has been openly confiding in her husband at every juncture, and that Richard has been tracking the affair with eager interest. This dialogue of astonishing revelation is the culmination of act 1, in which Richard acts the part of Grand Inquisitor catechizing Bertha relentlessly, and once again insisting on her right to "free choice" when she asks if she should keep the appointment at the cottage. He is calculating, sardonic, coolly casual, and haughty, even capable of righteous indignation, as he cross-examines her, denouncing Robert as "a liar, a thief, and a fool! . . . A common thief! . . . My great friend! A patriot too! . . . A thief—nothing else! . . . But a fool also!" (*E* 63). Once the audience is aware of Richard's prior knowledge, the parting between the two men echoes with heightened irony:

ROBERT
Good afternoon, Richard. We shall meet tonight.

RICHARD
[*Touches his hand.*] At Philippi. (*E* 54)

And the interim conversation between Richard and his son, once Robert had left, can now be fully appreciated for its ironic reverberations:

RICHARD

But when you give it, you have given it. No robber can take it from you. . . . It is yours then for ever when you have given it. It will be yours always. That is to give.

ARCHIE

But, pappie?

RICHARD

Yes?

ARCHIE

How could a robber rob a cow? Everyone would see him. In the night, perhaps?

RICHARD

In the night, yes. (*E* 56)

The cross-questioning of Bertha reveals a Richard capable of exacting his pound of flesh, but at this moment of exalted triumph, denouncing Robert and threatening to pursue him with his denunciation, Richard slips and gives Bertha her long-sought advantage:

BERTHA

. . . I see it all!

RICHARD

[*Turning.*] Eh!

BERTHA

[*Hotly.*] The work of a devil!

RICHARD

He?

BERTHA

[*Turning on him.*] No, you! The work of a devil to turn him against me. (*E* 64)

Once Bertha "turns," the advantage is and remains hers until the curtain. She accuses him of turning Archie against her, of never having loved his own mother, of going out on "rambles in the rain," neglecting her and the child, of taking advantage of her "simplicity," and of establishing a relationship with Beatrice that is deterimental to Bertha. "I believe you will get very little from her in return," she says prophetically, corroborating the sense the audience attained from the conversation between Richard and Beatrice: "Because she is not generous and they are not generous." When she asks him,

"Is it all wrong what I am saying?," Bertha must be aware of the success of her counteroffensive, and Richard can only concede (*"darkly"*), "No. Not at all" (*E* 69). There remains only the realization that he has, in the intensity of the situation, forgotten his promise to Archie to ask Bertha whether he may go out with the milkman in the morning, and he disguises his "betrayal" by granting the permission without consulting her.

Act 2 is clinical and classical in its economy and precision: in the Ranelagh cottage the three principals converge (minus Beatrice, Archie, and Brigid) for what has all the possibilities of a showdown. The setting suggests both a confining enclosure of claustrophobic intensity and a remoteness from the Merrion parlor where one feels that home life, a workplace, and a neighborhood alleviate the tensions of the love affair. Yet there is a comic touch to the bachelor's lair in which Robert awaits his prey, playing Wagner on the piano and spraying the room with perfume in tense anticipation— and comic irony in the appearance of Richard in lieu of Bertha. The scheme to get Richard out of the way by arranging the dinner at the vice-chancellor's has backfired for Robert, but he attempts both to put a good face on it and get Richard out before Bertha arrives. Richard dallies with him for only a few moments before leveling his accusations and revealing his full knowledge. The initiative is certainly his, and Robert has litle choice but to capitulate and at least feign contrition. It is a fascinating display of Richard's serene vindictiveness, and yet somehow the balance of power unmistakably shifts halfway through: "What a lesson! Richard, I cannot tell you what a relief it is to me that you have spoken—that the danger is passed. Yes, yes. [*Somewhat diffidently.*] Because ... there was some danger for you, too, if you think. Was there not?" (*E* 77). (Throughout *Exiles* Joyce shows himself skillful in the crafting of his stage directions and the placement of his ellipses.)

Robert has invariably revealed himself as a bumbler, Richard the prestidigitator, yet Robert cannot but be credited with knowing exactly what he is now doing in manipulating the counters, in turning disaster into a stalemate from which he can maneuver more easily than his adversary. He follows up his disconcerting question by speaking *"bravely,"* presumably congratulating Richard on speaking out before it proved too late, "Until I had come to like her more and more (because I can assure you it is only a lightheaded idea of mine), to like her deeply, to love her. Would you have spoken to me then as you have just now? [RICHARD *is silent*. ROBERT *goes on more boldly.*] It would have been different, would it not?" (*E* 77). What Robert eventually proposes is a competition between them ("A duel—between us?", Richard asks, almost with incredulity):

ROBERT

[*With growing excitement.*] A battle of both our souls, different as they are, against all that is false in them and in the world. A battle of your soul against the spectre of fidelity, of mine against the spectre of friendship. All life is a conquest, the victory of human passion over the commandments of cowardice. Will you, Richard? Have you the courage? Even if it shatters to atoms the friendship between us, even if it breaks up for ever the last illusion in your own life? (*E* 89)

That this sort of "romantic" sophistry can actually prevail against Richard's "classical" casuistry seems incredible, yet Robert has softened up his opponent before throwing down the gauntlet by flattering Richard's strength, playing on his self-doubt, insisting on the doctrine of a woman's free choice that Richard himself had advanced, and giving him plenty of opportunity to confess his own feelings of guilt regarding Bertha. Richard never quite accedes to the duel, but has trapped himself into a laissez-faire position: "Together no. Fight your part alone. I will not free you. Leave me to fight mine" (*E* 90).

Onto this field of disarray Bertha makes her entrance, first confronting her husband and then her prospective lover. The men have so whittled away at each other that both are easy marks for her serene strength. The nominal trophy of their contention, Bertha has a will of her own, dealing first with Richard, while Robert hides in the rainy garden. Richard's triumph in bearding the lion in his den she reduces to insignificance: "I knew you could not remain away. You see, after all you are like other men. You had to come. You are jealous like the others." And even his masculine assertion ("I had to protect you from that") she dismisses with ease: "That I could have done myself" (E 92). Her self-assurance, however, is anything but ironclad, and in an indecisive moment she pleads, "Why do you not defend me then against him? ... Dick, my God, tell me what you wish me to do?" But that is precisely what Richard Rowan cannot do. The compact with Robert that he had backed himself into prevents him from making decisions for anyone but himself. "There is something wiser than wisdom in your heart," he tells her, and allows her to make her own way. "I will remain," she says—*"dreamily"* (E 96).

With the rain-drenched and apprehensive Robert she plays both the role of the solicitous mother and the coy seductress, bringing him back to at least a semblance of his self-esteem and allowing the atmospherics of romantic seduction to sustain itself in the love cottage. Her self-possession may in fact give Bertha a false sense of security, for Robert has as his subtle weapon the evidence of Richard's abdication, the acquiescence for a duel that shifts the battle to the center of the court:

ROBERT

... He has left us alone here at night, at this hour, because he longs to know it—he longs to be delivered.

BERTHA

From what?

ROBERT

[*Moves closer to her and presses her arm as he speaks.*] From every law, Bertha, from every bond. All his life he has sought to deliver himself. Every chain but one he has broken and that one we are to break, Bertha—you and I. (E 112)

Transformed once again into the cat in command, Robert makes his play, assisted by wind and rain and encroaching darkness, and the second act ends with Bertha hovering on the brink of capitulation.

The suspended moments at the close of act 2 result in the ambiguous resolutions of the final act, an inconclusiveness that is characteristic of almost all of Joyce's narrative closures from "The Dead" through *A Portrait, Ulysses,* and *Finnegans Wake.* Determining the consequences of the romantic interlude in the cottage dominates the cat-and-mouse situation in act 3, but even that issue must take a back seat because of the early morning arrival of Beatrice Justice. Although she presumably intrudes to bring the good news of the article on Richard Rowan in the morning newspaper, she also inadvertently contributes to the suspense by mentioning Robert's arrival home late last night and his packing for an imminent departure. Bertha takes the opportunity to confront Beatrice, shifting the subject from Robert to Richard, and behind the façade of polite conversation the battle lines are drawn: Bertha implies that Beatrice exerts a hold on Richard, and Beatrice suggests that Bertha has pulled Robert into her sphere. The first round results in a standoff, Beatrice just barely holding her own against Bertha's directness. They are temporarily interrupted by Richard, who sardonically reads the leading article and quickly leaves, abandoning the arena once again to the two women.

The second round takes up where the first left off, but it is immediately apparent that Bertha does not intend to renew her attack. Instead, she confesses her sorrows to Bertha ("I gave up everything for him, religion, family, my own peace"), staunchly maintaining her refusal to be humbled: "I am very proud of myself, if you want to know. . . . I made him a man. . . . He can despise me, too, like the rest of them—now. And you can despise me. But you will never humble me, any of you." Her moment of defiance is capped with an offer of friendship with her presumed rival, an allegiance that transcends their rivalry for Richard:

BERTHA

[*Going to her impulsively.*] I am in such suffering. Excuse me if I was rude. I want us to be friends. [*She holds out her hands.*] Will you?

BEATRICE

[*Taking her hands.*] Gladly. (*E* 129-30)

The gesture of feminine solidarity consolidates Bertha's position as she returns her focus to the men who have viewed her as their domesticated mouse. Robert has been sent for, preventing his inconspicuous escape, but Bertha first faces Richard alone in the wake of the clouded events of the night before. Although she insists that she will tell him the truth, Richard is equally insistent that he will never know the truth, reiterating that he is as always willing to allow Bertha her complete freedom. The chilling ambiguity of truth (the suspicion that the curtain which shrouded the later events in the Ranelagh cottage will remain impenetrable) presents itself in a self-negating conundrum: "I will tell you the truth, Dick, as I always told you. I never lied to you" (*E* 133), but we also remember her words to Robert in the previous scene: "But, you see, I could not keep things secret from Dick. Besides, what is the good? They always come out in the end" (*E* 103). Is the truth for Bertha to disclose or for Richard to uncover? Can she tell it or must he find it for himself?

If she intended to make her statement now, she is once again interrupted, this time by the farewell visit of Robert Hand, and it is he who makes the "official" declaration. Bertha gets to deal with him first, so that whatever "secret" is shared by the two of them as their private domain cannot help but be revealed in their open and unobserved discussion. Yet the "truth" retains its pristine ambiguity even between them:

ROBERT

Has he asked . . . what happened?

BERTHA

[*Joining her hands in despair.*] No. He refuses to ask me anything. He says he will never know.

ROBERT

[*Nods gravely.*] Richard is right there. He is always right. (*E* 137)

Bertha determines that it is for Robert to make their statement to Richard, but the confused lover balks when she insists on "The truth! Everything!"—his feelings of guilt ostensibly tantamount to a confession. Yet even Robert seems unaware of the reality of objective truth:

ROBERT

[*Catching her hands.*] Bertha! What happened last night? What is the truth that I am to tell? [*He gazes earnestly into her eyes.*] Were you mine in that sacred night of love? Or have I dreamed it?

BERTHA

[*Smiles faintly.*] Remember your dream of me. You dreamed that I was yours last night.

ROBERT

And that is the truth—a dream? That is what I am to tell?

BERTHA

Yes.

ROBERT

[*Kisses both her hands.*] Bertha! [*In a softer voice.*] In all my life only that dream is real. I forget the rest. [*He kisses her hands again.*] And now I can tell him the truth. (*E* 137-38)

Exiles as a document of "stage realism" comes into question with this unusual exchange during the moments of "resolution": the privileging of dream over truth (or the identification of dream *as* truth) disturbs the complacency of verisimilitude in Joyce's drama and focuses on evanescent qualities stronger than its adherence to literal reality. The dream aura sustains itself and expands in the revelation scene despite the efforts of the prosaic Robert to reassure his friend ("I failed. She is yours, as she was nine years ago, when you met her first" [*E* 139]— here there is no attempt to correct the singular to the plural). The pervasive atmosphere of functional unreality is established at the opening of their interview by an intrusive "Fishwoman" hawking her wares along the road outside, overheard in the Rowan house: "Fresh Dublin bay herrings!" (*E* 139). Nothing in *Exiles* quite prepares us for this blatant interference of external and unrelated reality, making something as mundane as a fish vendor an element of mysterious inclusion.

In the closing moments of the play the circumference narrows down to an intimate exchange between Richard and Bertha (Beatrice neutralized; Archie having had his ride on the milk wagon; Robert's departure for Surrey paralleling Beatrice's initial arrival from Youghal). The universe is theirs alone, and it is Bertha who has gathered all of the controlling strings in her hands, not only insisting on her fidelity toward him, but on a continuous and unbroken fidelity. She couples her present devotion to the years of his unfaithfulness: "Heavens, what I suffered then—when we lived in Rome! . . . I was alone, Dick, forgotten by you and by all" (*E* 145). The question that she asks is a compound without separate entities, so that it is the total construct of her allegiance that is under examination: "do you believe now that I have been true to you? Last night and always?" (*E* 144). The doubt that Richard Rowan insists upon seems as permanent as Bertha's devotion, but is enclosed within and subsumed by that devotion as she contains both past and present in her mastery of the situation:

BERTHA

I am yours. [*In a whisper.*] If I died this moment, I am yours.

RICHARD

[*Still gazing at her and speaking as if to an absent person.*] I have wounded my soul for you—a deep wound of doubt which can never be healed. I can never know, never in this world. I do not wish to know or to believe. I do not care. It is not in the darkness of belief that I desire you. But in restless living wounding doubt. To hold you by no bonds, even of love, to be united with you in body and soul in utter nakedness—for this I longed. And now I am tired for a while, Bertha. My wound tires me. [*He stretches himself out wearily along the lounge.* BERTHA *holds his hand, still speaking very softly.*]

BERTHA

Forget me, Dick. Forget me and love me again as you did the first time. I want my lover. To meet him, to go to him, to give myself to him. You, Dick. O, my strange wild lover, come back to me again! [*She closes her eyes.*] (*E* 147)

In the final conflict of cat-and-mouse, the wounded cat luxuriously stretches himself out in weariness and is ministered to by his prey.

The culmination of their tensions brings the Rowans to a stasis in a drama marked by its nontragedy, a drama of "convalescence," of wounds that neither heal nor destroy. Richard Rowan had initiated a collison course for himself and those he assumes he controls, and the duration of the drama is a period in which the collision is both inevitable and prevented. The real action of the play had taken place in the past: the consequences of the exile from Ireland and Richard's exiling of himself from Bertha are what *Exiles* depicts. Beatrice carries her exile with her at all times, an incomplete woman, a convalescent with no chance of complete health, a Protestant in a Catholic enclave. Robert had exile thrust upon him as he abandons the field of inconsequence for a retreat to Surrey, designating as his heir Richard's son: "Perhaps, there, Richard, is the freedom we seek—you in one way, I in another. In him and not in us" (*E* 143). And the freedom that Richard seeks and presumably grants so freely locks him into permanent exile whether in or away from Ireland. Bertha, on the other hand, forced by Richard into exile from her religion, family, and own peace of mind, exiled from him in Rome and from her proper status upon return to Ireland, not only refuses to allow herself to be humbled, but brings everyone around her to heel. As Joyce's complete woman she has the power to wound and to nurse, free to choose and consequently to make demands. An expansion on the Gretta Conroy of "The Dead," she anticipates the creation of the Molly Bloom of *Ulysses* and the Anna Livia Plurabelle of *Finnegans Wake*.

Despite Joyce's economy of style and form in *Exiles,* the play seems unable to contain itself with-in the walls of the stage set or the time of the three acts, and Joyce's Notes (which since 1951 have been appended to all printed versions of the play) hint at a broader drama that transcends the stage scenario. Even the stage directions, sparse and pointed as they are, suggest an inner drama, a drama of variant possibilities, within the text. A glance at the cast of characters reveals an alliterative pattern of the names of the two men and the two women, as well as charactonymic potentials: the earthiness of Bertha, Robert as robber-thief, the richness of Richard, and Beatrice as the Dante guide (even Brigid as Irish goddess and patron saint). Surnames loom as large: the significance of the rowan tree in Irish mythology, the arch commentary on Justice (as different from Mercy), and the obviousness of Hand— primary implement of taking, touching, robbing (there are over a hundred references to *hands* in the stage directions, mostly in relation to Robert). In crafting his drama Joyce concerned himself with the language of gesture, but was no less conscious of language itself: a symbolic web of possibilities exists outside the dialogue of *Exiles,* adding a dimension often lost in stage production.

5

The Dublin Odyssey

Fragments Toward a Mosaic

Nothing that Joyce had as yet written or published (*Chamber Music, Dubliners, A Portrait of the Artist as a Young Man, Exiles*), or anything that anyone else had as yet published (including T. S. Eliot's *Prufrock and Other Observations,* 1917), could prepare the English-reading world for *Ulysses.* Joyce himself made various efforts of preparation, including the serial publication of successive chapters—a preparation that was dramatically short-circuited when the League for the Suppression of Vice in America successfully went to court to stop the publication of *Ulysses* in *The Little Review.* Notoriety was now destined to plague Joyce's new work, and the problem of a publisher became acute, until Sylvia Beach contracted to enter the publishing business (for Joyce only) and use her Shakespeare and Company bookshop imprint for the 1922 publication of *Ulysses*—and arranged for a French printer in Dijon to set the type. (Joyce had already experienced the burning of his *Dubliners* manuscript by an irate printer in Dublin, and it was preferable in this case that the typesetters did not read English.) The publication in Paris in 1922 of *Ulysses*, along with the appearance of Eliot's *The Waste Land*, marks that year as the focal point of High Modernism in twentieth-century English-language literature.

For Joyce the transition from his previous writing into *Ulysses* was smooth and natural: during the delays in the publishing of *Dubliners*—which allowed for the addition of "The Dead"—he had contemplated another short story to be called "Ulysses" for inclusion, a story idea that contained the germ for the seven-hundred-page novel. Joyce already had a significant number of fictional Dubliners in motion, and a quasi-autobiographical artist as a young man at the stage in his life when he was about to encounter "the reality of experience" (*AP* 253)—"for the millionth time," but also in a sense for the first time as an adult. The amalgam of the world of *Dubliners* and the extended persona of Stephen Dedalus needed only one or two structural devices for the development of Joyce's new fiction, but Joyce had by now envisioned a far more complex format in which to capture the modern world, and compounded numerous structural devices for his *Ulysses*. The most basic structure was the consolidation of his materials into a single day in the city of Dublin and its environs (Thursday, 16 June 1904), a day that has been tagged (perhaps too facilely) as "the dailiest day possible." The most elaborate structure was the use of Homer's *Odyssey* as an underlying format for a depiction of a very nonheroic day in an equally nonheroic world, with an "Odysseus" figure who was apparently very much an ordinary citizen, hardly more than the typical man in the street. Despite the presence of Stephen Dedalus once again, it is Leopold Bloom—as well as his memorable wife, Molly—who is at the center of the Odyssean epic of James Joyce's contemporary world.

Joyce's use of formal structures, reflected in the schema that he prepared for his biographer and for analysts of *Ulysses*, was nonetheless undercut by his imaginative virtuosity as a writer. Although Dublin is the focal center of the novel, the first three chapters (and one later one) take place several miles outside the city, beginning with the coastal town of Sandycove, where Stephen is now temporarily resident in an old fortification tower leased by the British government, and working as a schoolmaster (also temporarily) in the nearby town of Dalkey. Dublin *and environs* provide the locus, and the time frame is also as inexact: the first four morning hours are compressed into the first three chapters, with one hour missing, and these hours are duplicated—with Bloom instead of Stephen as protagonist—in the next three chapters. Thereafter, from noon on, the hours move along consecutively—except for a two-hour gap in the early evening—culminating close to 3 A.M. on Friday, 17 June. The flow of time, like the firm situation in space, is subject to certain variations, disruptions, and faulty transitions, almost a human variable introduced to dislocate the fixed patterns that control the tightly organized elements of the text. Human fallibility is invariably operative in Joyce's epic that is also a mock epic, but nonetheless epical.

The relationship between Joyce's *Ulysses* and Homer's *Odyssey* is signaled primarily in Joyce's book title, and even that allows for a certain distancing—the use of the Roman name immediately suggests a "translation" in language, culture, and geography from the original Greek. Joyce reduced Homer's twenty-four books of *The Odyssey* to eighteen chapters, and one of those deals with material that Homer had specifically avoided, passages through the unpredictable "wandering rocks." The patterning of a three-part text follows the Homeric mold: the three opening chapters dealing exclusively with Stephen comprise the Telemachia; the central twelve chapters focusing primarily on Bloom, but bringing Stephen into a relationship with Bloom, form the Odyssey proper; and the last three chapters, which return Bloom to his home at number 7 Eccles Street, with Stephen in tow, parallel the Nostos. Joyce had originally designated each of his eighteen chapters with a title from Homer (and these were in actual use when *Ulysses* was being serialized), but they were deleted once the book was put into print. Nonetheless, they are still employed by critics of *Ulysses* as a convenience:

Telemachus, Nestor, and Proteus (The Telemachia); Calypso, Lotus Eaters, Hades, Aeolus, Lestrygonians, Scylla and Charybdis, Wandering Rocks, Sirens, Cyclops, Nausicaa, Oxen of the Sun, and Circe (The Odyssey); Eumaeus, Ithaca, and Penelope (The Nostos). The centrality of Homer's text to that of James Joyce has been stressed by some readers, the parody of a heroic epic in a novel of the mundane world by other readers, and the mere casualness of associations by still others. Odysseus's Descent into the Underworld allows for a funeral cortege through Dublin on its way to bury Paddy Dignam in the Glasnevin cemetery, with constant references to the extended route as "a fine old custom" that "has not died out" (U 88), to the less interesting side of Sackville Street as the "dead side of the street" (U 95), to an untenanted house with an unweeded garden as a "place gone to hell" (U 100). As Bloom hungrily wends his way toward lunch in Lestrygonians, hundreds of words suggesting food crop up in the oddest but apparently natural ways: observing the city marshal he thinks, "Look at the woebegone walk of him. Eaten a bad egg. Poached eyes on ghost" (U 165). The cannibalism of Homer's Lestrygonians is replicated in an unsanitary eatery where Bloom notices "That fellow ramming a knifeful of cabbage down as if his life depended on it. . . . Give me the fidgets to look. . . . Tear it limb from limb" (U 170).

The most minute incidents of *The Odyssey* provide a world of associations for Joyce, many of them ironically comic, as he "wrote over" Homer's material without ever losing the thread of his own Dublin narrative. Stephen and Bloom are not father and son, so that Stephen's pose as a Telemachus in search of his father is tangential, although he has certainly disassociated himself from the Simon Dedalus whom he caustically labels his "consubstantial" father, and yet he accurately mimics his "consubstantial father's voice" (U 38), and finds himself both a storyteller and a drunkard on 16 June 1904. Bloom as Odysseus has no living son to meet again; his only male child, Rudy, had died almost eleven years ago at the age of eleven days, but his loneliness for a younger male companion to talk with leads him to befriend the son of the Simon Dedalus with whom he shared a carriage to Dignam's interment. As a faithful wife like Penelope, Molly Bloom has often been considered a travesty, since not only does she have an adulterous affair with Blazes Boylan on this particular day, but a list of twenty-five extramarital "lovers" is revealed late in the book and has been taken literally by many readers as evidence of her promiscuous infidelity. A careful analysis of the names on that list discloses the ludicrousness of associating more than one or two of them as even possibilities, and even those seem remote. So the famously unfaithful Molly may well have been an exact parallel for Penelope, at least until the afternoon when Boylan comes rapping at her door. And although her own thoughts, the sometimes quite ordinary but sometimes quite erotic thoughts that make up the entire last chapter of *Ulysses,* reflect on a majority of the men on the list in ways that make them highly unlikely as past lovers, there are references (and amorous ones) about a Lieutenant Stanley Gardner who is not among the names. The list, after all, seems to be dependent on the jealous mind of Molly's husband, composed of names she let drop and people he himself knows, so that the absence of Stanley Gardner indicates that Leopold Bloom has no idea of the existence of that now-dead former "lover." Molly Bloom will forever hover between fidelity and infidelity, a true Penelope and a parody of her.

For many readers Joyce's most delightful use (and misuse) of Homer resides in the Cyclops chapter, where Joyce places his "Odysseus" uncomfortably in Barney Kiernan's pub (Bloom is no drinker), a hostile environment in which an overly athletic Irish chauvinist known as "the citizen" looms large, holds forth at length, and drinks at the expense of others. The nondrinking Bloom accepts a cigar instead of a drink, and the cigar itself mirrors in diminished proportions that tree trunk that Odysseus had ignited at one end and used to gouge out the single eye of the gigantic Polyphemus. The others in the pub are not Bloom's "men" at all, as the other captives had been Odysseus's, but almost all are in some way hostile toward him, since some of them believe that Bloom has won an enormous sum on the Gold Cup race and still avoids standing drinks. Bloom eventually escapes the ire of the giant-citizen, fleeing in a horse-drawn carriage, although a biscuit tin is hurled after him, missing him apparently because the sun temporarily blinded the enraged citizen. Odysseus's deception in giving his name as Noman is prismatically reflected throughout the chapter, where often no names are given or pseudonyms used, so that not only is the citizen nameless throughout, but the narrator of this particular chapter, a new character in the book who takes it upon himself to record in his own distinctive voice the events in Barney Kiernan's pub, is only known as a "collector of bad and doubtful debts" (*U* 292), and later referred to as *"The Nameless One"* (*U* 586). He rambles along in his prejudiced way, using the colorfully scatological argot of a Dublin barfly, in telling his story of Bloom's experiences in the pub, but his narration is frequently interrupted by inserted passages of hyperbolic parody, exaggerated commentary in various journalistic and legalistic forms that parallel the "real" text, elements of giganticism in language that remind us that the Cyclopes were a race of giants. The single-minded focus of the citizen's xenophobic championing of his own race reminds us that Polyphemus had only one eye—and Odysseus rid him of that one. Consequently, the opening sentence of the chapter encapsulates so much of all this: "I was just passing the time of day with old Troy of the D. M. P. at the corner of Arbour hill there and damned but a bloody sweep came along and he near drove his gear into my eye" (*U* 292)—a sentence that begins egocentrically with an "I" and ends with another "eye." "Ay, says I" (*U* 292) accentuates the tension between the monocular and the binocular.

Ulysses is simultaneously a comic and a cosmic novel, and *The Odyssey* is not the only parallel text that tracks the events in the lives of Stephen Dedalus, the Blooms, and the other Dublin citizens. Leopold Bloom has his analogues in Moses, Christ, Elijah, the Wandering Jew, Sinbad the Sailor, as well as

Odysseus, while Stephen is at times recognizable in his role as Hamlet, Icarus, Siegfried, Lucifer, the Prodigal Son, as well as Telemachus (late in the book Stephen and Bloom will look into the same mirror and see the magical reflection of William Shakespeare). Molly is the Virgin Mary, the Daughter of the Regiment, Gea-Tellus the Earth Mother, and the Wife of Bath. Most of these associations are subtle and even tenuous, and in many ways these three principal characters in the novel are some of the most realistically drawn characters in literary fiction. And it is on the literal, and even naturalistic, level that *Ulysses* has its primary existence: the complex allusive system and the various other structural and stylistic innovations that distinguish *Ulysses* as a revolutionary and modernistic work are firmly established on that basic plot level. Although the modernist movement developed the nearly plotless novel, *Ulysses* nonetheless has its fully developed (although nonheroic) story line.

The story of Stephen Dedalus begun in *A Portrait of the Artist* is carried over into *Ulysses* after a break of a year or two, and then frozen into a tableau of that single day in his life. In the interim he has been to Paris as a student, pulled back into the Dublin net by the impending death of his mother:

a blue French telegram, curiosity to show:
—Mother dying come home father. (*U* 42)

And although, as we later learn, his mother's death occurred almost a year ago, he is still mired in his Dublin environment, none too pleased by the prospects of remaining there, and haunted by the memories of his dead mother. The parental home is in pathetic disarray, his father pawning household items to support his life in pubs and his sisters dependent on charity for their food, but Stephen has wrenched himself free and now finds himself sharing the Martello tower with its renter, Malachi (Buck) Mulligan. Discontent with this arrangement, both because he mistrusts the overtures of the egregious Buck and dislikes the Englishman Haines whom Mulligan now has staying with them, Stephen begrudgingly gives up the key to the tower to Mulligan, and departs for the day, first to his teaching position and later for his social life in the city, determined not to return: "I will not sleep here tonight. Home also I cannot go" (*U* 23). Dispossessed of his native soil Stephen Dedalus feels himself to be already an exile from Ireland. Mulligan he pinpoints at various stages during the morning and in the early afternoon with three single words, uttered in the privacy of his own thoughts as maledictions: "Chrysostomos," "Usurper," "Catamite" (*U* 3, 23, 204), as if by such labels Mulligan can be exorcised.

The exorcism of May Goulding Dedalus from Stephen's guilt-ridden consciousness preoccupies him throughout the day, and may actually have been achieved in the postmidnight hour. Accused by Mulligan of having refused to pray at his dying mother's bedside, the apostate Stephen, who still wears black in mourning her death the previous June, carries her decaying image with him. Mulligan is relentless in his accusation:

—The aunt thinks you killed your mother, he said. That's why she won't let me have anything to do with you.

—Someone killed her, Stephen said gloomily.

—You could have knelt down, damn it, Kinch, when your dying mother asked you, Buck Mulligan said. I'm hyperborean as much as you. But to think of your mother begging you with her last breath to kneel down and pray for her. And you refused. There is something sinister in you. (*U* 5)

Left alone Stephen involuntarily conjures up his mother's ghost, with "glazing eyes, staring out of death, to shake and bend my soul" (*U* 10), and he cries out against death and her avenging spirit:

Ghoul! Chewer of corpses!
No mother. Let me be and let me live. (*U* 10)

Stephen's morning is a rather disconcerting one, as he disentangles himself from Mulligan and Haines, as he defers both to the students over whom he has no real control and to the headmaster, Mr. Deasy, a pro-British Unionist and casual anti-Semite who persists in lecturing him while doling out the monthly salary. Only in the third chapter, as Stephen walks along the beach at Sandymount and is alone with his highly convoluted thoughts, does he reach a measure of equilibrium, and even attempts to compose a quatrain of verse on a torn portion of Mr. Deasy's letter to the newspapers on foot-and-mouth disease. The glimpses one gets of Stephen in the early afternoon are at a newspaper office and the National Library; in both cases he is acting as messenger for Deasy, but in each he holds forth to those assembled, in narrating a "Parable of the Plums" that he has been composing in his mind, and in presenting his theories on Shakespeare to the librarians and literati. He has purposely avoided his appointment with Mulligan and Haines, standing drinks instead to the hangers-on from the newspaper office, but Mulligan nonetheless arrives at the library to interrupt his pontifications on the Bard ("Hast thou found me, O mine enemy?" he thinks [*U* 197]). At mid-afternoon Stephen can be seen browsing among the bookstalls, where he encounters one of his younger sisters and tries to harden himself to the obviously miserable plight of the Dedalus children. But thereafter he disappears from sight, making the round of the pubs all day, until he is found late in the evening at the Lying-In hospital commons room, seriously drunk and still drinking, so that when the last pub closes he and his companion Lynch seek refuge in Bella Cohen's brothel in the "nighttown" section of Dublin. Now under the watchful eye of the solicitous Bloom, who has followed him from the hospital in concern for his safety, Stephen experiences a hallucinatory encounter with his mother's ghost: he lashes out at it with his walking stick, smashing Bella Cohen's chandelier shade. "Cancer did it, not I," he pleads (*U* 580), but in defiance shouts, "Break my spirit all of you if you can! I'll bring you all to heel!" (*U* 582). After the smashing of the lamp, no specter returns to haunt Stephen during the remainder of the long night.

The Stephen narrative becomes peripheral after the third chapter of *Ulysses* and is subsumed by the vast wealth of narrative involving Leopold Bloom. Joyce explained that Stephen has a form that could not be changed (his fixed existence deriving from *A Portrait*) and that his hero now was Bloom—much to the chagrin of such fierce intellectuals as Ezra Pound, who preferred the focus on the artist-protagonist. The blatantly ordinary Bloom is not only the corporeal counterpart to Stephen's cerebral component, but as the catechism in the Ithaca chapter characterizes:

What two temperaments did they individually represent?
The scientific. The artistic. (*U* 683)

The differentiation is an important one, but within the context of *Ulysses* is also somewhat ironic. We have observed Stephen in his artistic guise during the day, a relatively free one for him since it is a half day in the academic week, and he does a great deal more talking and drinking than writing (the quatrain composed on the beach is mostly an unconscious plagiarism, and Stephen himself challenges the meaning imposed by the rhyme words). There seems to be a significant gap in his capacity for artistic performance, which Stephen offhandedly attributes to his forgetting to help himself to library slips on which to write. But if Stephen's identification as representative of the artistic temperament is imperfect, Bloom as an exemplar of the scientific temperament is equally inexact. He does display an active curiosity in astronomy, wonders what parallax means, and explains thunder (a teleological terror to Stephen) as merely "a natural phenomenon" (*U* 395), yet one suspects that not only a lack of advanced formal education, but also a tendency to accept untested theories and even superstitions mars his scientific pose. As the day wears on and the thoughts and actions of Leopold Bloom contribute to a compound portrait of the character, complex facets lead to a understanding of him as a decent and intelligent human being (Joyce referred to him as a "good" man), but certain deep-seated contradictions also slowly emerge. He does, after all, carry a shriveled potato in his pocket, given to him by his mother as a protective against disease, mockingly exalted as a "Potato Preservative against Plague and Pestilence" (*U* 499).

The thousands of inconsequential things that we learn about Leopold Bloom in the course of *Ulysses* coexist almost inseparably from the dozens of vital pieces of information, and it is sometimes a matter of choice as to which are germane to the character and which are general aspects of the ordinary human being. That "Mr Leopold Bloom ate with relish the inner organs of beasts and fowls" (*U* 54-55) is only the first of such introductory items, and they build up in no logical order of selectivity, but only as he moves through his ordinary day. He works as an advertisement canvasser for the *Freeman's Journal*—the latest in a series of jobs he has held in Dublin for more than a score of years—and consequently roams rather casually around the city, presumably in pursuit of advertisements, generally as footloose as Stephen on this day, if not as fancy-free. (Most of the masculine population of Dublin that we meet in *Ulysses*, members of its bourgeois class by and large, are equally desultory, alighting for longest periods of time in public houses with drinks in hand. It is a somewhat unusual day since one of Bloom's casual acquaintances is being buried between 11 A.M. and noon, a fitting excuse for several Dublin males to take at least part of the day off (none of them seems a particularly close friend of the deceased Dignam). In the newspaper office just after the funeral Bloom encounters several of the "mourners" and thinks, "Ned Lambert is taking a day off I see. Rather upsets a man's day a funeral does" (*U* 124), and to a great extent he himself is doing much the same thing. The unsuccessful pursuit of a single ad for Alexander Keyes, tea merchant, has him looking for a design in an old newspaper in the library, and trying to contact the newspaper foreman. Like Stephen's ramblings, Bloom's wanderings over the city are characteristic of a rather leisurely society in tranquil times, relatively relaxed on a sunny day in June during an uneventful period of Irish history, a predominantly masculine society that spends its time strolling about, drinking pints, talking endlessly and often maliciously, and singing sentimental songs.

Although he blends into the Dublin background and tries to remain unobtrusive, Leopold Bloom is an anomalous character in that world. Born of a Jewish father from Hungary who had converted to the Church of Ireland before Leopold's birth, he has since himself converted to Roman Catholicism when he married Marion Tweedy some sixteen years ago. Yet it is apparent from his equal ignorance of Judaism, Protestantism, and Catholicism that Bloom is estranged from all three religions, but has them all as a part of his individual heritage— an Everyman who is also a Noman. He has no close friends, and remembers back to the early days of his marriage when several acquaintances from the Jewish quarter of the city were part of a social circle in which he moved. His loneliness is intensified by the absence of a male offspring, and he seems on occasion to seek out the companionship of a young man with whom he can establish an intellectual friendship, a surrogate father-son relationship. But, essentially a loner and careful to avoid rebuff, Bloom does not pursue the matter very actively. Something of a mysterious figure despite his ordinariness, Bloom invites various kinds of speculation: about his finances ("He doesn't buy cream on the ads he picks up" [U 177]) and his role as a Mason ("He's in the craft" [U 177]); about his sexual proclivities ("O, I fear me," says Mulligan, "he is Greeker than the Greeks" [U 201]); his patriotism and national allegiance ("What is your nation if I may ask, says the citizen" [U 331]); and of course his religion ("He's a perverted jew" [U 337]). Along with the suspicion and mistrust there is also a measure of begrudging respect and even an exaggerated sense of awe: "it was he drew up all the plans according to the Hungarian system," claims Martin Cunningham (U 337), crediting Bloom with providing the idea of Sinn Fein to the nationalist leader, Arthur Griffith. And Lenehan, although no known authority on the subject, can claim that "There's a touch of the artist about old Bloom" (U 235). Despite the sorry state of Bloom's marriage, and the willingness of his detractors to question his sexual potency, there is still no rumor in Dublin that Bloom is a cuckold—a condition that he himself is aware of as taking place that very evening in his home at 7 Eccles Street, a condition that has him wandering about the city and reluctant to return home until the coast is clear.

As the minute pieces of evidence accumulate during the course of a long and involved narrative, the problem of the Bloom marriage takes on various shades and dimensions. Late in *Ulysses* we learn that there has been a lapse of "10 years, 5 months and 18 days during which carnal intercourse had been incomplete, without ejaculation of semen within the natural female organ" (*U* 736)—that is, since five weeks before the birth of Rudy. Readers have jumped to various conclusions: that there have been no sexual activities between husband and wife for that entire period, and/or that Bloom was sexually impotent, and of course that Molly was compensatorily promiscuous. The finer shadings of meaning, however, are significantly different: Bloom has remained sexually attentive and active, but has been careful to avoid *completed* intercourse, and Molly complains in her revery thoughts of remaining unsatisfied by her husband's sexual performances. Bloom, on the other hand, has quite probably "arranged" the affair for Molly with Blazes Boylan that culminates on this day, having introduced them to each other despite his thoughts as he sees Boylan from the window of the funeral carriage: "Is there anything more in him that they she sees? [sic] Worst man in Dublin" (*U* 92). He has also arranged for Milly Bloom, although only fifteen years old, to be apprenticed to a photographer in Mullingar, so that the Bloom house is empty during the day. Boylan, a promoter and impresario, has undertaken a concert tour for Molly, and his morning letter to her announces that he will be calling on her (apparently at four in the afternoon), bringing the program for the concert. In gossipy Dublin the word is out about Molly's scheduled tour, as Bloom himself informs those who ask about Molly, and then has to indicate that Boylan is arranging the tour. He remains vague when C. P. M'Coy asks, "Who's getting it up?" (*U* 75), but when Nosey Flynn later asks exactly the same question, Bloom's hedging is ineffective: "Ay, now I remember.... Isn't Blazes Boylan mixed up in it?" (*U* 172). Boylan's musical enterprise is already known to the barflies at Barney Kiernan's and Bloom admits that "He's an excellent man to organise. Excellent" (*U* 319), so that the anonymous collector of bad debts jumps to the conclusion: "Hoho begob, says I to myself, says I. . . . Blazes doing the tootle on the flute" (*U* 319).

The Nameless One's surmise is the closest that anyone in Dublin comes to knowing about the Boylan affair, nor is there any previous rumor of an unfaithful Molly circulating in the city, despite the various comments on her ample and tempting physical proportions. Lenehan boasts to M'Coy that during a carriage ride shared with the Blooms, "I was tucking the rug under her and settling her boa all the time. Know what I mean?" (*U* 234), which Molly corroborates with the curt dismissal: "he was making free with me after the Glencree dinner coming back that long joult over the featherbed mountain" (*U* 750). Various males have occasion to comment on Mrs. Bloom in their characteristic ways, so that even the proportions of her physical ampleness are as diverse as there are witnesses. John Henry Menton's recollections of her are further back in the past than Lenehan's, but essentially substantiate the praise ("She was a finelooking woman. I danced with her, wait, fifteen seventeen golden years ago, at Mat Dillon's in Roundtown. And a good armful she was" [*U* 106]). The disgruntled barfly in Barney Kiernan's, however, is contemptuous about Molly: "The fat heap he married is a nice old phenomenon with a back on her like a ballalley" (*U* 305). The Molly Bloom that we meet on 16 June is a thirty-three-year-old soprano, married for sixteen years but increasingly more dissatisfied with her husband's sexual inadequacies, and embarked on a blatantly sexual affair, perhaps her first infidelity, with no romantic illusions, and an active affection and even sincere respect for her cuckolded husband. Bloom's compliance with her liaison with Boylan exists as a major mystery to most readers, as does his oblique sexual proclivities

The Bloom we encounter somewhat resembles the stereotypical man who has been married to the same woman for many years and is approaching middle age, hesitantly pursuing sexual adventures that are more hypothetical than real, too cautious to take dangerous risks. Buying his breakfast kidney at the pork butcher's he sees the next-door servant girl and hopes "to catch up and walk behind her if she went slowly, behind her moving hams" (*U* 59), but she turns the wrong way and he does not bother to follow. The morning hours before the funeral are taken up with collecting a clandestine letter from a typist named Martha Clifford, with whom he has recently begun exchanging coyly erotic letters, using a pseudonym, Henry Flower. Bloom weaves his way circuitously through the Dublin streets by an indirect path to the post office where he shows his Henry Flower card and gets Martha's latest letter. He reads it surreptitiously, and although titillated by its suggestiveness he remains determined not to arrange an assignation as she requests, and even considers employing the letter as stimulation for masturbation in the Turkish bath. But, although in the bath he regards his "limp father of thousands, a languid floating flower" (*U* 86), he does not masturbate at the time. As darkness falls that evening, however, he voyeuristically enjoys the sights of the raised skirts of Gerty MacDowell, who is watching the fireworks, and this time he takes advantage of the darkness to masturbate inside his clothes, commenting to himself: "Damned glad I didn't do it in the bath this morning over her silly I will punish you letter" (*U* 368). In Bella Cohen's brothel after midnight Bloom pays his ten shillings and pays flirtatious attention to the prostitute Zoe, but his interest is exclusively in protecting the drunken Stephen, whom he follows out of the house without either of them receiving the usual compensations for their payments.

Given this degree of sexual interest and activity, the mystery of Bloom's mismanagement of his conjugal sexuality deepens, especially since Molly is so often in his thoughts throughout the day. The commission he anticipates from the Keyes advertisement he contemplates spending on intimate presents for Molly, and the approach of the time for her assignation finds him progressively uneasy. During the morning hours he tries to focus only on the time of the funeral, but during the afternoon he cannot keep from anticipating the assignation. When he spies Boylan from the carriage, Bloom can quickly look away, inspecting his fingernails, but after lunch he almost walks into him, rushing ahead to avoid a confrontation and remembering the planned call at 7 Eccles Street ("Afternoon she said" [U 183]). As four o'clock approaches, he becomes even more anxious ("Not yet. At four, she said. Time ever passing. Clockhands turning" [U 260]). To Bloom's astonishment, just before the hour of four, he sees Boylan drive up to the Ormond Hotel bar ("It is. Third time. Coincidence" [U 263]), and is so fascinated that he follows him into the Ormond, selecting to eat an early dinner in the company of Richie Goulding so that he can observe his rival from the restaurant without himself being seen. Boylan has a sloe gin and converses with Lenehan, and eventually drives off to arrive at Molly's door somewhat late, as Bloom "hears" the sound of the jaunting car all the way to Eccles Street and Boylan's assertive knock at the door. And as he eats his meal and addresses a money order to Martha, Bloom imagines the moment and the intensity of the consummation of the Molly/Boylan affair—far too soon, as it turns out.

Molly's thoughts as she dozes in the morning hours are quite specific about Boylan's performance as a lover, and become even excessively so as her annoyance with her husband increases: "he must have come 3 or 4 times with that tremendous big red brute of a thing he has," she muses (U 742), later maintaining that it was "4 or 5 times locked in each others arms" (U 763) and "5 or 6 times handrunning" (U 780). Her exasperation with Poldy seems specific ("its a wonder Im not an old shrivelled hag before my time living with him so cold never embracing me except sometimes when hes asleep the wrong end of me not knowing I suppose who he has any man thatd kiss a womans bottom Id throw my hat at him after that hed kiss anything unnatural" [*U* 777]), yet there are diverse aspects to her disgruntlement. She is aware of his philandering, crediting the timid Poldy with more than he ever allows himself. As she anticipates the resumption of the Boylan affair on the tour in Belfast, she is grateful that her husband will be at his father's grave site instead: "suppose our rooms at the hotel were beside each other and any fooling around went on in the new bed I couldnt tell him to stop and not bother me with him in the next room . . . then he wouldnt believe next day we didnt do something its all very well a husband but you cant fool a lover after me telling him we never did anything of course he didnt believe me" (*U* 747-48). Molly acknowledges the existence of Poldy's attentions, but also acknowledges her profound disappointment.

Bloom has for almost eleven years been insisting on various sexual practices that remain "incomplete, without ejaculation of semen within the natural female organ," obviously avoiding conception. For a father who mourns the loss of his only male child and sadly feels the absence of a male heir, Bloom himself has been responsible for preventing the birth of a successor to the dead Rudy. The supposition builds up in *Ulysses* that little Rudy had been born deformed. Bloom remembers the reaction of the midwife to the birth of the child, "She knew from the first poor little Rudy wouldn't live. Well, God is good, sir. She knew at once" (*U* 66); "Meant nothing. Mistake of nature" (*U* 96), he muses at the cemetery. Molly corroborates Rudy's unfortunate birth: "what was the good in going into mourning for what was neither one thing nor the other" (*U* 774). The death of the boy has certainly changed Bloom's life, and he admits to himself that sex with Molly has never been as pleasurable since the death. Ned Lambert emphasizes the change by recalling the Bloom of eleven years ago: "you should have seen Bloom before that son of his that died was born. I met him one day in the south city markets buying a tin of Neave's food six weeks before the wife was delivered" (*U* 338). The decision not to engender another child was obviously Bloom's, apparently never discussed with Molly, and was

probably due to Bloom's belief that he as the father was the
cause of the child's unfortunate condition. "If it's healthy it's
from the mother," he tells himself at the cemetery, "If not the
man" (*U* 96). Despite his scientific temperament and belief in
natural phenomena, Bloom has held on to this unscientific
superstition and allowed it to dominate his life and disastrously
affect his marriage with Molly.

Molly Bloom emerges from a shadowy existence in an
otherwise predominantly male world in the Penelope chapter
of *Ulysses* as an extraordinary person who assumes impressive
stature as she weaves her thoughts through recollections and
fantasies, dislikes and desires. Her final words before sleep,
"yes I will Yes" (*U* 983), are a reaffirmation of her submission
both to the man who became her husband and the first man
who kissed her beneath the Moorish walls of Gibraltar, and are
interpreted widely as an affirmation of life, as well as an aspect
of feminine submissiveness—a contradiction that Molly easily
subsumes within her expansive personality. The final yes also
counterbalances her first utterance of the morning, a muffled
negative when asked if she wanted anything besides toast and
tea for breakfast: "Mn" (*U* 56). Bloom during the course of the
day remembers Molly at various stages of their life together,
from their first meeting through the years of their marriage,
especially the happier days before Rudy's death, and the
Lenehans and Mentons remember her as well. Once Bloom
returns from the pork butcher's with his breakfast kidney and
sees Boylan's letter, thoughts about Molly (and Blazes Boylan)
are painful ones for him and her prefers to banish them
entirely—but without success. Before the arrival of the letter
he eagerly returns home, depressed that the sky has
momentarily clouded over: "To smell the gentle smoke of tea,
fume of the pan, sizzling butter. Be near her ample bedwarmed
flesh. Yes, yes" (*U* 61). After the funeral, as the hours lead
inexorably toward the hour of the assignation, a hungry Bloom
anticipates a hot lunch, but finds himself looking at lingerie in
a shop window:

Gleaming silks, petticoats on slim brass rails, rays of flat silk stockings.

Useless to go back. Had to be. Tell me all.

High voices. Sunwarm silk. Jingling harnesses. All for a woman, home and houses, silk webs, silver, rich fruits, spicy from Jaffa. Agendath Netaim. Wealth of the world.

A warm human plumpness settled down on his brain. His brain yielded. Perfume of embraces all him assailed. With hungered flesh obscurely, he mutely craved to adore.

Duke street. Here we are. Must eat. The Burton. Feel better then. (*U* 168)

A hot meal becomes his only means of solace now that Molly's "bedwarmed flesh" is not a source of comfort, but the disgusting eating habits at the Burton restaurant dissuade him from entering, and he settles for a cold sandwich at Davy Byrne's pub instead. Toward 4 P.M., Bloom already contemplates his dinner ("Eat first. I want. Not yet. At four, she said.... On. Where eat? ... Eat. If I net five guineas with those ads. The violet silk petticoats. Not yet" [*U* 260-61]), his thoughts an amalgam of the Boylan affair, the desire for food, and the lingerie that he intends to buy for Molly on the commission to be gained from the Keyes ad. At the Ormond he hears Boylan depart for 7 Eccles Street and imagines the seduction taking place in his home, while he devours grilled liver and mashed potatoes.

Between the Calypso chapter and the Penelope chapter Molly Bloom is hardly seen at all, except for a brief instance when a one-legged sailor comes begging under the windows of Eccles Street: "A plump bare generous arm shone, was seen, held forth from a white petticoatbodice and taut shiftstraps. A woman's hand flung forth a coin over the area railings" (*U* 226). In the interim between Molly in bed at her breakfast and Molly in bed when Bloom finally returns home in the small hours of the morning, she has been up cleaning the house, changing the sheets and moving the furniture, preparing herself for Boylan's arrival, and although the delivery of the program for the concert was primarily an excuse, Molly did rehearse her rendition of "Love's Old Sweet Song" before the seduction. As a professional singer Molly has a life and a career of her own, and at one time in her marriage was the sole support of the family, singing in a temperance hall when Bloom had lost his job. Although impressed with Boylan's energetic performance as a lover, Molly is displeased by his overly familiar behavior ("pulling off his shoes and trousers there on the chair before me so barefaced without even asking permission" [*U* 776])—not to mention his slapping her bottom. And although it is clear that in many ways she prefers her gentle and considerate Poldy, the Boylan affair will continue on into the Belfast tour.

Nonetheless, a new possibility has arisen for Molly since her husband brought Stephen Dedalus home at one in the morning: despite Stephen's refusal to spend the night at 7 Eccles Street, the possibility has been introduced that he will return in the near future. With everything up in the air after the early morning hours of 17 June, speculation is rife: Bloom would like the intellectual companionship of the young "scholar," and seems willing to offer him a room at 7 Eccles Street, from which vantage point Stephen could give Molly Italian lessons in exchange for singing lessons. This typically fanciful Bloomian idea is paralleled by Molly's conjectures about Stephen as a potential lover, a replacement for the rather egregious Blazes that would meet with Poldy's approval. She remembers little Stephen at ages five and eleven, and now imagines him as "a handsome young poet" (*U* 776) whom she could sexually educate, although she worries that he might have "long greasy hair hanging into his eyes or standing up like a red Indian" or that he might be "that stuck up university student sort" (*U* 775). Just as the conjectured Stephen appeals to Molly's vanity and sexuality, he also appeals to her maternal concern:

they dont know what it is to be a woman and a mother how could they where would they all of them be if they hadnt all a mother to look after them what I never had thats why I suppose hes running wild now out at night away from his books and studies and not living at home on account of the usual rowy house I suppose well its a poor case that those who have a fine son like that theyre not satisfied and I none. (*U* 778)

(Despite the dense pattern of Molly's meandering thoughts, only a handful of clues regarding her own background becomes available: growing up in Gibraltar in the care of an Irish father, Brian Cooper Tweedy, who may have been a major, but more probably a sergeant major, and a Jewish-Spanish mother, Lunita Laredo, who apparently faded out of her life when Molly was born.)

The "night world" of *Ulysses,* somewhat anticipating that of *Finnegans Wake,* sharply differentiates from the daylight existences of Bloom and Stephen and the other denizens of Dublin. As darkness descends on this warm sunny day in mid-June, Bloom finds himself alone along the beach at Sandymount (where Stephen has strolled before noon on his way into the city), having visited Paddy Dignam's widow and assisted in adjusting the problem with her husband's lapsed insurance. He had been invited out there by Martin Cunningham and John Wyse Nolan, not from any excess of friendship for Bloom but because his expertise as a former insurance agent could be exploited, and at dusk he is still in Sandymount, his companions having apparently returned to town without him. As Gerty MacDowell leans back further and further to watch the fireworks display, Bloom is aroused by the view of her thighs, but once she gets up to leave he notices that she is lame. Darkness had not fallen quickly enough to allow her to limp away unnoticed, and in the depression following his ejaculation he drowses a bit against the sea wall. "My fireworks," he muses, "Up like a rocket, down like a stick" (*U* 371). Emerging from his reveries he attempts to write with a stick in the sand (on the same beach where Stephen had earlier proclaimed, "Signatures of all things am I here to read, seaspawn and seawrack" [*U* 37]). Bloom momentarily considers writing a message, presumably to Gerty, beginning, "I. . . . AM. A. . . ."—only to realize:

No room. Let it go.

Mr Bloom effaced the letters with his slow boot. Hopeless thing sand. Nothing grows in it. All fades. . . .

He flung his wooden pen away. The stick fell in silted sand, stuck. Now if you were trying to do that for a week on end you couldn't. Chance. (*U* 381-82)

Bloom's sexual parabola, from tumescence to detumescence, reasserts itself in this "chance" retumescence, but Molly (as in so many instances) has the last word: "O Poldy, Poldy, you are a poor old stick in the mud! Go and see life. See the wide world" (*U* 440).

The world of Dublin in which he has been navigating a careful and sober path has had its hazards during daylight hours: in crossing the street he avoids "the loose cellarflap of number seventyfive" (*U* 57), and when he is talking to Mrs. Breen on Westmoreland Street, he draws her out of the path of a demented stroller well known to him ("—Watch him, Mr Bloom said. He always walks outside the lampposts. Watch!" [*U* 159]). At the intersection of Dawson and Molesworth Streets Bloom assists a blind stripling safely across the street, but his navigational skills and watchful caution are sorely missed when the blind youth and the demented walker collide in the Wandering Rocks section, ironically under the window of the dental offices of a "Mr Bloom" (*U* 250). The night world is more hazardous, and having whiled away the early evening and being too late to attend the theater, Bloom chooses a safe course and visits the National Maternity Hospital where an acquaintance, Mrs. Mina Purefoy, has been in labor for three days. In the commons room he joins the medical staff and students, and their friends, including a drunken Stephen whom he feels needs watching and guiding, and so undertakes to remain with the group when they move to the nearest pub for more drinks before closing time. Thereafter, the course is a treacherous one: Stephen allows Lynch to lure him to "nighttown," the red-light district across the river. An altercation at the train station between Stephen and Mulligan, observed by Bloom but never clearly explained, apparently spells the end of the "friendship" between the two. As Bloom thinks of it: "the very unpleasant scene at Westland Row terminus when it was perfectly evident that the other two, Mulligan, that is, and that English tourist friend of his, who eventually euchred their third companion, were patently trying, as if the whole bally station belonged to them, to give Stephen the slip in the confusion" (*U* 620). Bloom loses Stephen at the station, and consequently arrives in nighttown at the witching hour in a concerned hope of picking up his trail in that dangerous terrain. Even crossing a street is risky, and with a stitch in his side Bloom runs in the path of a sandstrewer, emerging safely. "Close shave that," he comments, "but cured the stitch" (*U* 435).

Inadvertently Bloom nears the house in which Stephen and Lynch are being entertained by prostitutes Florrie and Kitty, and is himself accosted by Zoe Higgins, who asks, "Are you looking for someone? He's inside with his friend." Her guess is more than mere coincidence, and she even asks, "(*Suspiciously.*) You're not his father, are you?" The clue is simply that Stephen and Bloom are "both in black" (*U* 475), Bloom having dressed appropriately for Dignam's funeral and Stephen still in mourning for his mother. As disparate as these two citizens of Dublin so apparently are, this small link has its significant element, especially since Zoe leaps to the conclusion that they might be father and son. (Bloom had earlier wondered whether he might not have fathered a son during his first sexual encounter with Bridie Kelly, who he now imagines is a prostitute in nighttown; and Stephen, who had also speculated on the chance of having engendered a child, has already dismissed paternity as a "legal fiction" [*U* 207].) Despite the differences in education and intellectual sophistication, both Bloom and Stephen are interested in Shakespeare, certainly a common heritage to many people in the English-speaking world, but this is almost a mystical bond between them, so that in the hallucinatory confines of Bella Cohen's brothel they see themselves in Shakespeare's image: "*Stephen and Bloom gaze in the mirror. The face of William*

Shakespeare, beardless, appears there" (*U* 567). Both have an involvement in music that may not be directly professional (Stephen has actually turned his back on a singing career), but is sufficient to suggest to Bloom the idea of having Molly tutor Stephen. Perhaps even more symbolically apt is the keyless situation that both of them find themselves in on 16 June 1904: Stephen has had to surrender the key to the Martello tower to Mulligan on a ruse (although, after all, Mulligan did pay the rent); and because he was wearing his black suit for the funeral, Bloom had left his latchkey in his other trousers, and has to let himself down into the areaway to gain access to his house through the kitchen door. As outsiders in their native city of Dublin, Stephen and Bloom are keyless citizens by more than just inadvertence.

The perils of nighttown prove painfully real for Stephen, despite Bloom's attempts at protecting him. In his drunken disequilibrium Stephen encounters the image of his dead mother and shatters Bella Cohen's chandelier shade in lashing out at the specter. While Bloom mollifies Mrs. Cohen and pays for the shade, Stephen has run into the street and ostensibly insulted Cissy Caffrey, whose soldier escort, Private Carr, drunkenly undertakes to assuage her honor and manages to knock the shaky Stephen down. Bloom seems unable then to protect Stephen from the suspicious Night Watch, although Corny Kelleher, undertaker and police informer, intercedes to prevent the arrest, and Bloom is left to minister to the comatose young man. In the Eumaeus chapter he leads him to a cabman's shelter for sustenance, but cannot get him to eat or drink the coffee there. Stephen is generally unfriendly, or at least uncommunicative, in the face of Bloom's constant conversation, and the environment of the cabman's shelter takes on its own sinister characteristics, so that Bloom decides to lead Stephen out of it and take him to his own house, for "a cup of Epps's cocoa and a shakedown for the night plus the use of a rug or two and overcoat doubled into a pillow" (*U* 657-58). On the way out Stephen comes out of his torpor sufficiently to ask a seemingly banal question:

—One thing I never understood, he said, to be original on the spur of the moment, why they put tables upside down at night, I mean chairs upside down on the tables in cafes.

To which impromptu the never failing Bloom replied without a moment's hesitation, saying straight off:

—To sweep the floor in the morning. (*U* 660)

In some strange way this conversation appears to break the ice between them; perhaps something in the simple, basic common sense of Leopold Bloom has appealed to the highly over-intellectualized Stephen Dedalus, for thereafter they establish a rapport, and converse together (about Shakespeare, for one subject). Stephen even allows Bloom to take his arm (which he refused to allow Mulligan) as they wend their way, Bloom guiding him past a "sweeper car" and the "three smoking globes of turd" mired by the horse (*U* 665), the two resembling to the driver a married couple arm in arm.

Whatever real rapport is established between the two in the kitchen of 7 Eccles Street is a tenuous one, and probably a temporary one. They drink cocoa together, "in jocoserious silence," and because Epps's is identified as a "massproduct, the creature cocoa" (*U* 677), the "jocoserious" assumption of a communion is often made; they continue to discuss a wide variety of subjects, establish the coincidence of mutual acquaintances, share information even where neither is particularly an expert (in the writing of Irish and Hebrew, for example), and are generally in accord and in good humor. If there is an element of discord it occurs when Stephen sings a medieval ballad, of Little Harry Hughes and the Jew's Daughter, the anti-Semitic implications of which leave Bloom "sad" and "silent" (*U* 692), but do not really disturb his equilibrium, and the incident is smoothly passed over. It can be assumed that Stephen's "gaffe" was either unwitting or perhaps even calculated to reestablish a degree of distance between himself and his new acquaintance, a reminder that his creed of silence, exile, and cunning is still operative, and that he is carefully mistrustful still of all offers of friendship. The Cranly who had worked his way under Stephen's guard in *A*

Portrait, only to supplant him in Emma's affections, is only a spectral recollection, as when Mulligan that morning "suddenly linked his arm in Stephen's," and Stephen thought, "Cranly's arm. His arm" (*U* 7). Mulligan himself became the next betrayer, as witness the incident at Westland Row terminus. And Lynch had quickly deserted Stephen when the contretemps with Private Carr began, so that Stephen denounced him as his Judas: "—And that one was Judas, said Stephen" (*U* 615). Stephen politely turns down the "shakedown" offered by Bloom, and leaves 7 Eccles Street for destinations unknown, but not before the two urinate together in the back garden under Molly's lighted window and under a "heaventree of stars" (*U* 698). Stephen had already announced that he would soon give up his job at Mr. Deasy's school, and consequently can in the end be viewed as jobless, homeless, friendless, practically penniless. But he has met and shared several hours on 16/17 June with that ordinary but unique Leopold Bloom, and heard about Molly Bloom as well.

Crossing Eighteen Bridges

Every reading of *Ulysses* prepares us for a rereading, as we carefully store away in our minds the bits and pieces that form various patterns which are assembled and reassembled. *Ulysses* exists simultaneously as the sum of its parts, that larger design that conjures up Homer and Dante and Shakespeare, Dublin topography and Irish history, and the inner design that concerns itself with fictional people and their lives. Joyce referred to the eighteen chapters of his novel as eighteen bridges, and as the styles change from chapter to chapter, the unique experience of each becomes more significant. Yet, the constant that remains beneath cosmic significance and stylistic innovation is the story of Molly and Leopold Bloom, and of Stephen Dedalus, and of numerous minor Dubliners as well. It is a story skillfully told, although often obliquely told, and a story always worth retelling.

The somewhat cryptic and often elliptical events of *Ulysses,* and the concentrated characterization of the principal figures and diffuse meanderings of the minor ones, are buried within the folds of a novel that concerns itself more with its manner of presentation than the materials presented. Each of the chapters develops a style of its own, and if the differences between the early ones (what Joyce once termed the "initial" style) seem minimal, the abrupt changes in the later ones are overwhelming. That the opening of *Ulysses* deposits the reader without ceremony atop a Martello tower, where a shaving Mulligan performs a mock Mass for his own edification, is hardly as disruptive as the early intrusion of internalized monologue within the consciousness of Stephen Dedalus. "Chrysostomos," thinks Stephen (*U* 3), as he looks into the gold points of Mulligan's teeth and listens to his glib patter, ironically conjuring up the golden-mouthed Church father, St. John Chrysostomos—and we later find that the Buck's full name may well be "Malachi Roland St John Mulligan" (*U* 417). The sudden intrusions become almost a commonplace as Stephen conjures up remembered scenes from the past, free-associates as his mood carries him, makes mental notes, and takes stock of situations and attitudes, not just at the quiet moments when he is alone at the gunwale of the tower, but even during conversations with Mulligan and Haines. His departure from the tower toward Dalkey frees him from the uncomfortable circumstances of being dependent on Buck's hospitality and subject to his offensive possessiveness and Haines's violent nightmares. In his mind he dismisses the Englishman with the time-honored Irish examples of treachery, "Horn of a bull, hoof of a horse, smile of a Saxon," as well as categorizing with pinpoint accuracy the dominating Mulligan: "Usurper" (*U* 23).

Once out of the confines of his "peers" Stephen faces the disquieting trap of the schoolhouse, where his affluent students are dolts and his teaching abilities minimal, particularly since he has no skill in controlling the class, much less directing them. He blunders through, sympathizing with the pathetic student who reminds him of himself as child, and when class ends, he enters Mr. Deasy's study to receive his salary and endure Deasy's pontifications and prejudices. The Stephen who was sleepy and disgruntled in the first chapter is politely deferential now, and only in the privacy of his own thoughts does he allow full expansion to his attitudes as he accepts his employer's letters to the press for delivery. "Mulligan will dub me a new name," he speculates, "the bullockbefriending bard" (*U* 36). Self-irony helps him survive such uncomfortable situations in which he is forced to be polite to his superior (just as it had when dealing with his pupils, presumably his inferiors). In a necessarily quiet voice he attempts to counter the older man's contentions: to the anti-Semitic assertion that "England is in the hands of the jews," he suggests that a "merchant . . . is one who buys cheap and sells dear, jew or gentile, is he not?" (*U* 33-34). The oblique observation and the overly subtle but quietly understated barb are his overt defense against Deasy, but the sanctity of his private thoughts afford him the greater pleasure for cunning cleverness. As Stephen emerges from the schoolhouse, he passes "the lions couchant on the pillars" of the gate, and labels them as "toothless terrors" (*U* 35-36), a designation that applies to Deasy as well. And although Deasy has the last word—and presumably the last laugh—baiting the departing Stephen with his jest that Ireland never persecuted the Jews "because she never let them in" (*U* 36), the chapter closes with what appears to be a narrative observation but is actually Stephen's on the penny-pinching Deasy: "On his wise shoulders through the checkerwork of leaves the sun flung spangles, dancing coins" (*U* 36). Even at this early stage of the complex stylistics of *Ulysses* it can be observed that a constant interaction betwen external narration and internal monologue has been effected, and the constant eroding away of the distance between exterior and interior flow of narrative and stream of consciousness becomes heightened as the book progresses into greater complexities.

With the third chapter, the last one in which Stephen dominates completely, the outer world of "antagonists" fades away for a brief respite, as he is seen totally alone strolling along Sandymount Strand on his way into Dublin. And very much alone with his own thoughts, so that external narration, like external reality, has very little impact upon him, and his thoughts dominate almost all of the scene. He passes a pair of women whom he assumes are midwives (and will later fictionalize in his Parable of the Plums), a couple of gypsies picking cockles, a live dog and the carcass of a dead dog; he surreptitiously picks his nose and urinates against a rock, and he jots down the four lines of verse that come as an inspiration. Otherwise, his thoughts meander like the trickles of seawater veining the beach, or loom up in chaotic bits of ideas or remembered items from his schooling, like the shells and flotsam along the strand. For a while he considers visiting the Gouldings, his aunt and uncle on his mother's side, and we may even conjecture that the reason he is walking through Sandymount, rather than having taken the train all the way into Dublin, is to arrange a place to stay. But as he walks along, the imaginative Stephen Dedalus hypothesizes what such a visit would be like—on the basis probably of many previous visits—and in his mind he "writes" a delightful vignette, beginning, "I pull the wheezy bell of their shuttered cottage: and wait. They take me for a dun, peer out from a coign of vantage" (*U* 38). The Goulding household scene utilizes Simon Dedalus's caustic verbal wit, Stephen's borrowings from Shakespearean verbiage, highly realistic details from ordinary life, and an ironic perspective to allow for a narration that reveals the meager skeletons in the Goulding closet just as they are in the process of cleverly concealing them. There is no surprise, therefore, that Stephen in his thoughtful trance walks past the Goulding cottage and keeps on walking toward Dublin: the visualized scene has a greater reality than any visit could rival. By contrast with this finely honed piece of mental fiction, the pale-vampire poem seems pale indeed, and perhaps the direction of Stephen's literary talent is being subtly signaled by the juxtaposition of the two within the Proteus chapter.

When time "begins again" with the fourth chapter, the interior monologue technique proves as pertinent to the new central character, Leopold Bloom, as it had for Stephen, although the language of Bloom's thoughts is as much conditioned by his spoken language as Stephen's had been by his own. "Another slice of bread and butter: three, four: right. She didn't like her plate full. Right" (*U* 55)—his thoughts as he prepares to serve Molly her breakfast in bed. Quick perceptions, immediate observations, rapid queries into things he does not understand, alert sightings of danger signals in the world around him, and nostalgic reflections of past events make up the pattern of Bloom's thoughts throughout his day, and although there is a solid stasis to his mood most of the time, he is easily affected by sad thoughts, unpleasant experiences, and even the sudden darkening of the sky. Cheered by a letter from daughter Milly, he is nonetheless disheartened by Boylan's communication to Molly, and his realization that the inevitable is finally occurring on this particular day. After buying and cooking and eating his own breakfast he prepares to defecate in the outdoor jakes in his uncultivated garden, taking with him a copy of a popular periodical, *Titbits,* where he reads a prizewinning story and thinks that he can do as well. "Might manage a sketch," he reflects, and even adds Molly as a coauthor, "By Mr and Mrs L. M. Bloom" (*U* 69), although later that evening, after Molly's affair with Boylan has presumably begun and been consummated, another urge toward literary accomplishment finds him less generous in sharing the credit: "*The Mystery Man on the Beach,* prize titbit story by Mr Leopold Bloom. Payment at the rate of one guinea per column" (*U* 376). The image of the "mystery man"—a gentleman taking his constitutional stroll along the strand—reminds Bloom of Dignam's funeral that morning, just as the sound of the church bells that he hears upon emerging from the jakes seem to him to sound the death knell for Paddy Dignam. "Poor Dignam!" he muses (*U* 70).

The next hour, in which Bloom departs from 7 Eccles Street, and begins his walk through the city, is missing from the text, and the opening of the "Lotus Eaters" chapter locates him already in central Dublin along the quays. As we track him along his way, a rather purposeful aimlessness seems to direct his steps, as if he had eaten of the lotus of forgetfulness. If his destination is the post office at which he expects to get Martha Clifford's amorous letter, he is going out of his way, heading in the wrong direction until he backtracks—as if to shake off anyone who might be trailing him. Once he has the letter he encounters C. P. M'Coy, whom he finally rids himself of, perhaps having noted the pathetic parallels with himself (M'Coy also has a wife who sings, and he himself has also held various jobs—Bloom encounters various such "ghosts" during the day). He reads the letter in a deserted back street, amused at Martha's eagerness, coy sensuality, and grammatical mistakes ("do not deny my request before my patience are exhausted" [*U* 78]). He rests awhile in All Hallow's Church, having come through the back door, and exits through the front, off to Sweny's chemist shop to renew a lotion prescription for Molly and buy a cake of soap for his bath. This time he is waylaid by Bantam Lyons, eager to see the odds for the Gold Cup horse race in Bloom's copy of the *Freeman's Journal*. Intent on ridding himself of Lyons also, Bloom offers him the paper, saying, "I was just going to throw it away" (*U* 85). As a horse-race addict Lyons cannot resist the possibility of a mysteriously inadvertent tip, and resolutely marches off, determined to bet on the twenty-to-one outsider, Throwaway. That he later lets Lenehan talk him out of it costs him a windfall, and by closing time that night Lyons is observed by Lenehan as dangerously drunk. (Lenehan had also persuaded Boylan to bet on Sceptre, and has made yet another enemy with his "dead cert" [*U* 426].) By the end of the chapter Bloom is luxuriating in the Turkish bath, not the one on Tara Street that he originally intended, but the one near the chemist's shop, since he has probably run short of time in his elliptical wanderings and delays caused by M'Coy and Lyons. Indolence and forgetfulness are his for the moment at least, and he will actually forget to return to the chemist's to pick up Molly's lotion and pay for the soap.

The funeral procession in the Hades chapter cuts a wide swath through Dublin, from the southeastern suburb of Sandymount to the northwestern cemetery in Glasnevin. The carriage that Bloom is in contains Simon Dedalus, Jack Power, and Martin Cunningham as well, and it should not be surprising that in their trek through Dublin they should see Stephen in Sandymount ("—Down with his aunt Sally, I suppose, Mr Dedalus said, the Goulding faction" [*U* 88]), and Blazes Boylan in front of a seafood restaurant (Molly assumes that "he must have eaten oysters I think a few dozen" for his sexual prowess [U 742]—but oysters would not have been available in June). The sighting of Boylan and the aura of death affect Bloom's thoughts, and the mention of suicide as the "greatest disgrace to have in the family" and that "the man who does it is a coward" (*U* 96) further disturbs Bloom, whose father had poisoned himself in despondency. And thoughts of the dead Rudy are never far from his mind. Only Martin Cunningham seems to know about Bloom's father, and he tries to offset the harsh judgments by Power and Dedalus, and once they are out of the carriage he lectures them on their faux pas, in the first instance in the novel where a narrative exists *outside* the active experience or the inner thoughts of the two main characters. Yet all of the gloom of the deadly surroundings and the concomitant associations do not seriously alter Leopold Bloom's basic cheerfulness, and his thoughts are not without a touch of morbid humor. He even finds himself listening to the "music" of the coffin-cart wheels until he stops himself from humming: "The ree the ra the ree the ra the roo. Lord, I mustn't lilt here" (*U* 104). As he counts the mourners, he realizes that they are an unlucky thirteen, one of whom, a stranger in a mackintosh, becomes a nagging minor mystery throughout *Ulysses*. Joe Hynes is covering the funeral for the *Evening Telegraph,* and assumes from Bloom's comment on the raincoat that the stranger's name is "M'Intosh" (*U* 112), and under that sobriquet he will appear in the newspaper that Bloom looks at late that night, along with other "mistakes," including "Stephen Dedalus B.A." (who was not there), "C. P. M'Coy" (whose name Bloom asked Hynes to include), "L. Boom" (a typo that annoys Bloom), and "M'Intosh" (*U* 647). A man in a mackintosh will make several sudden appearances throughout the day, but the one at the grave site also makes a sudden and mysterious disappearance: "Where has he disappeared to? Not a sign. Well of all the. . . . Become invisible. Good Lord, what became of him?" (*U* 112).

If the "Lotus Eaters" and "Hades" chapters have opened up the vista of the city streets, the "Aeolus" chapter extends that vista to include more Dubliners at points in their lives where Bloom and Stephen are only marginal presences. The gentlemen of the press and their hangers-on are at the center of this windy chapter of hot-air rhetoric, Bloom passing in and out in his professional capacity, and Stephen arriving somewhat later to offer to stand drinks and lead the press-gang to the pub, while narrating his parable. They manage to bypass each other without meeting, and Stephen also manages to avoid his father, who has left only moments earlier—and in effect *replaces* him as drinker and storyteller. The rhythmic movements of the presses and the opening and closing of doors parallel the shuttling to and fro of the characters, and Bloom notices the interaction of the mechanical and the human:

Sllt. The nethermost deck of the first machine jogged forwards its flyboard with sllt the first batch of quirefolded papers. Sllt. Almost human the way it sllt to call attention. Doing its level best to speak. That door too sllt creaking, asking to be shut. Everything speaks in its own way. Sllt. (*U* 121)

Bloom's observation that "everything speaks in its own way" has constant reverberations throughout *Ulysses*, and we become increasingly more aware of how Joyce's text speaks in *its* own way. In this newspaper-office chapter a series of bold-faced headlines or captions intrude at various junctures, averaging almost two to a page, and behaving very much as such capsulized signals do in a newspaper, calling attention. They begin in rather staid and dignified demeanor ("IN THE HEART OF THE HIBERNIAN METROPOLIS" [*U* 116]), but accelerate into a ghastly parody of jingoistic journalism: "DIMINISHED DIGITS PROVE TOO TITILLATING FOR FRISKY FRUMPS. ANNE WIMBLES, FLO WANGLES— YET CAN YOU BLAME THEM?" (*U* 150). These "eruptions" are all the more intrusive since they were added by Joyce after he finished writing *Ulysses*, as if as a reader he too heard the Aeolus chapter speak in its characteristic way.

The Lestrygonians chapter returns the focus to Bloom and brings the action once more into the city streets. His odyssey is now toward lunch, a respite both from unpleasant thoughts of home and the somewhat frustrating efforts to nail down the Keyes ad, and chance encounters once again make even the thoroughfares of one's own town slightly dangerous. First, a "sombre Y.M.C.A. young man . . . placed a throwaway in a hand of Mr Bloom" (*U* 151) that announces an evangelical meeting by a self-styled Elijah from Zion (Illinois), with whom Bloom obliquely identifies:

Bloo . . . Me? No.
Blood of the Lamb. (*U* 151)

He wads it up and throws the throwaway away, and it sails as skiff down the Liffey River, bobbing up occasionally like a wandering rock. As he passes the offices of the *Irish Times* Bloom remembers the innocent-sounding advertisement he had placed for a typist, and the subsequent correspondence with Martha Clifford that resulted from it, and it is here that he has his second encounter, with Josie Breen, once Molly's close friend. As with the M'Coys, Bloom sees the Breens as parallel lives with his own: Josie was once young and pretty, but is now a worried and slovenly wife, with a demented husband who is wandering the streets of Dublin threatening to sue someone who sent him a scurrilous postcard: "U.P.: up" (*U* 158). When Bloom reaches refuge at Davy Byrne's pub (after being driven out of the Burton Restaurant by "disgusting" eaters), he has to face an old acquaintance who also asks about Molly and mentions Boylan as well. No sooner has Bloom masterfully navigated the blind piano tuner across the street than he confronts the inevitability of running into Blazes Boylan head-on, and he dashes into the gates of the National Museum, hoping that the sun in Boylan's eyes prevented him from being seen. "Safe!" he announces to himself as he maneuvers behind the statues of the goddesses about whose anal orifices he had been curious, but the chance presence of Buck Mulligan on his way to the National Library prevents him from ascertaining the existence of such naturalistic detail. In a chapter in which the ingesting of food runs as a constant motif, "Lestrygonians" begins with a Christian Brother eating "scoopfuls of creams" and ends with the orifices of evacuation of Greek goddesses (*U* 151, 183), a complete alimentary progression.

The transition from the visceral to the cerebral is effected in the shift to Stephen once again and the location within the office of the librarian, where the subject is Shakespeare. Stephen's theories about Hamlet have been heard by Mulligan already, and in the Telemachus chapter he had quipped to Haines that Stephen "proves by algebra that Hamlet's grandson is Shakespeare's grandfather and that he himself is the ghost of his own father" (*U* 18). Haines is not now present, having gone instead to buy "Hyde's *Lovesongs of Connacht*" (*U* 186), the Celtophilic Englishman preferring translations from the Irish into English to a disquisition by an Irishman on the English national poet. Stephen's audience is dubious if not actually hostile, consisting of the poet-editor George Russell (to whom the foot-and-mouth-disease letter is delivered), and librarians Lyster, Best, and Eglinton—the chapter has more real persons from Joyce's Dublin, and references to many more real people, than any other in *Ulysses*. Eglinton is probably the most sceptical, but Stephen does a creditable job in neutralizing him; Lyster, the most sympathetic, but he is called away on library business twice, once by Bloom looking for the logo for the Keyes ad, and the other time by a priest who is working on an Irish-English dictionary. As Stephen meticulously argues his case, with guile and cunning and borrowed biographical information, he is interrupted by Mulligan, whom he was scheduled to meet earlier that afternoon but sent a telegram to instead. The Buck playfully cavorts about and attempts to steal the scene from Stephen, but not quite successfully. Stephen holds his own quite well against the odds, insisting that Shakespeare created life out of his own life and sublimated his own marital disaster into creative genius (a path Stephen seems to sense is inevitable for himself), and yet when asked if he actually believes his own theories, the ironic Stephen "promptly" says "No" (*U* 214), yet thinks of further substantiation that he wants to introduce. As he is being led out by Mulligan, who has momentarily snared him after all, they pass Leopold Bloom: "—The wandering jew, Buck Mulligan whispered with clown's awe. Did you see his eye? He looked upon you to lust after you. I fear thee, ancient mariner" (*U* 217). The second sighting of Boylan has now been matched with the second sighting of Stephen, as the antipodes of Bloom's concerns tighten toward a certain degree of resolution.

With "Wandering Rocks" a radically new departure becomes apparent, but serves for this chapter only: the larger cityscape of Dublin provides the setting, and a cross section of its citizenry the "heroes" and "heroines." Bloom and Stephen make their appearances, although only as two of many wandering rocks bobbing up unexpectedly in a series of isolated vignettes: Father Conmee travels on foot and by tram to arrange for schooling for one of the Dignam orphans; Corny Kelleher confers with a police constable; a one-legged sailor begs beneath Molly's window; three of the Dedalus girls cook soup in their kitchen; Blazes buys pears and peaches for Molly; Stephen is lectured on his abandoned musical career by his singing teacher; Boylan's secretary handles the office details; Ned Lambert shows Reverend Love an ancient historic site; Tom Rochford demonstrates his invention to Lenehan, M'Coy, and Nosey Flynn, and Lenehan tells M'Coy about Molly, after seeing Bloom at the bookseller's stalls; Bloom

rents a copy of *Sweets of Sin* for Molly; Dilly Dedalus waylays
her father outside the auction rooms and extracts a few
coppers from him; Tom Kernan strolls along, having booked
an order for tea and drunk a glass of gin; Stephen encounters
his sister Dilly at the bookstalls; Simon Dedalus meets his
friend Father Cowley; Martin Cunningham, Jack Power, and
John Wyse Nolan emerge from Dublin Castle and watch the
viceregal procession, which Kernan had just missed, pass by;
Mulligan and Haines take their midday refreshments in a cake
shop; the demented Farrell walks into the blind piano tuner;
orphaned Patsy Dignam looks at posters in shop windows;
and the viceregal cavalcade passes through Dublin on the way
to a bazaar where fireworks will be seen in the evening, viewed
by various citizens, including Richie Goulding, Simon Dedalus,
Reverend Love, Lenehan and M'Coy, Rochford and Flynn,
Dilly Dedalus, and Blazes Boylan—but not Stephen or Bloom.
The privilege of interior monologue, hitherto exclusive to
Stephen and Bloom, is extended in this "democratic" chapter
to four other characters, Father Conmee, Patsy Dignam, Tom
Kernan, and Boylan's secretary, Miss Dunne—the only time in
Ulysses that the thoughts of minor characters are conveyed
directly through the auspices of the internalized technique—
and if "Wandering Rocks" is a repository of many of the
dramatis personae already presented, it also offers advance
notices of such characters as Lydia Douce and Mina Kennedy
and Gerty MacDowell.

The Misses Douce and Kennedy are the "sirens" who serve
behind the Ormond Hotel bar in the following chapter, having
served as "intrusive" elements in the previous one, where
every section has one or more such intrusions from other
sections. Now in their proper place they cater to the needs of
Boylan and Lenehan, Simon Dedalus, Father Cowley, Ned
Lambert, Ben Dollard, and others, while Bloom and Richie
Goulding overhear them from the restaurant area. The
drinkers take turns at the piano for various songs, as music
makes itself a dominant factor in the Sirens chapter. Bloom is
sentimentally and erotically affected by the *"Co-me thou lost*

one!... Come!" climax of *M'Appari* (*U* 275), since Boylan has
since left the bar and his jaunting car was heard on its route
toward Molly. Bloom could even "hear" the jingle of that
jaunting car long after it was out of normal hearing, even to
the extent of "hearing" Boylan's impatient knocking on the
door of 7 Eccles Street: "with a loud proud knocker, with a cock
carracarracarra cock. Cockcock" (*U* 282). The soundwaves that
waft through the Ormond are as mysterious and unseen as
mental telepathy, so that the "musical" effects are preluded in
the opening pages as fragments of words and clauses that
become amplified progressively through the chapter as
coherent parts of the developing text. Even more enigmatic is
a reference to Shakespeare and his world that wafts through
just as Bloom is thinking about the Bard ("In Gerard's rosery
of Fetter lane he walks, greyed-auburn. One life is all. One
body. Do. But do" [*U* 280]), a fragment of Stephen's thought
in almost exact form from the Library chapter, having traveled
a mile or so in the past two hours. Bloom extricates himself
from the Ormond, convinced that Molly and Boylan have
consummated their affair as Simon sang his last *Come!* to
Martha. The blind stripling has tapped his way back to the
Ormond to retrieve his tuning fork, but Bloom is already down
the street, reading Robert Emmet's last words to the court,
holding back a flatulent impulse until the sound can be covered
by the noise of a passing tram:

Pprrpffrrppfff.
Done. (*U* 291)

The strangely unreliable method of narration in "Sirens," or
at least the unaccountability of intrusive information, might
prepare the reader for the surprising narrative voice in
"Cyclops," that anonymous barfly with a gift of gutter gab and
a spirit of meanness to match. The twenty-two instances of
parodic intrusions, however, are not as easily assimilated until
the reader enters into the fun of overextended parodies. In
many ways this is the most comic of all the chapters of *Ulysses,*
with its discussions of hanged men having erections and
drunken Bob Doran weeping over dead Paddy Dignam and

Alf Bergan convulsed over looney Denis Breen trying to sue someone over the "U.P.: up" postcard. It is also a seriously menacing chapter in which Bloom comes into open confrontation with the "Citizen" and risks physical violence as a result. Pubs are not Leopold Bloom's natural habitats (he does not drink and consequently does not stand drinks): he was safe enough in Davy Byrne's "moral pub" (*U* 171) for lunch, and remained in the dining area of the Ormond for his dinner. Now he finds himself at Barney Kiernan's, where he has arranged to meet Cunningham and Nolan in order to accompany them to the home of Dignam's widow. The timing is also unfortunate, since the habitues at Kiernan's speculate over the Throwaway win at Ascot. Bloom should never have actually ventured into the pub, or once inside not have stepped outside, allowing for the gossip behind his back. Public sentiment mounts against him insidiously, and he remains unaware of the source of the hostility. Nonetheless, he stands his ground and defends his rights to call Ireland his nation, even lecturing the assembled drinkers on humanitarianism:

—But it's no use, says he. Force, hatred, history, all that. That's not life for men and women, insult and hatred. And everybody knows that it's the very opposite of that that is really life.
—What? says Alf.
—Love, says Bloom. I mean the opposite of hatred. (*U* 333)

Bloom's statement is as poignant as it is awkward, and wasted on those who assume he has just won a fortune on a horse race and still avoids buying them drinks. Although fully aware that he has no real claims to being a Jew, he counters their anti-Semitism by asserting that "Mendelssohn was a jew and Karl Marx and Mercadante and Spinoza. And the Saviour was a jew and his father was a jew. Your God" (*U* 342), a contention hardly likely to endear him to his antagonists. The list itself is highly comic, since it includes Jews who had renounced Judaism, or been converted to Christianity, or been ex-communicated, except for Mercadante who was never a Jew—

but in his excitement Bloom has substituted his name for that of Meyerbeer, with whom he had earlier associated him. As he escapes the ire of the Citizen and the hurled biscuit tin, Bloom is comic-heroic in stature, and the elevated Biblical tone that records his departure soars momentarily, only to deflate into the tone of the caustic barfly:

And they beheld Him even Him, ben Bloom Elijah, amid clouds of angels ascend to the glory of the brightness at an angle of fortyfive degrees over Donohoe's in Little Green Street like a shot off a shovel. (U 345)

The presence of that involved first-person narrator in "Cyclops" gives way in the next chapter to third-person narration once again, but for the first half of "Nausicaa" the tone of that narration seems to derive from sentimental popular literature for Victorian women, full of overly discreet euphemisms, gushing romantic notions, and hypocritical saccharine avoidance of unpleasant realities. The narrative style ushers in and dominates the character of Gerty MacDowell, as she sits on a rock awaiting the pyrotechnics in the company of two other young girls, Edy Boardman and Cissy Caffrey, and the young siblings that they are presumably minding. Gerty's thoughts pour forth in a style that reflects the language of the literature she reads, and consequently her father's drunkenness becomes a topic for moral stricture and sympathy, the defection of a prospective wooer glossed over as occasioned by the boy's father's concern that he study for his examinations, and the attentions of the voyeuristic Bloom romanticized as the interest of a handsome dark stranger who probably has an unhappy home life. What the narrative style attempts to disguise is what Bloom learns when he watches her limp away into the descending darkness ("Tight boots? No. She's lame! O!" [U 367]). Retroactively the pieces reassemble themselves: Gerty is almost twenty-two years old, and the deflected "wooer" is apparently much younger, studying for his school exams; her concentration on dainty frills and housewifely amenities reveal her frustrated sexuality and a developing disappointment as a spinster. And we can easily assume that she is fully aware of her exhibitionism and Bloom's sexual appreciation of her naked limbs. As the chapter closes the narrative returns to a focus on Bloom's internalized night thoughts, the darker recesses of his moods, leavened by his philosophic equilibrium. He rehearses the day's events in his mind: "Long day I've had. Martha, the bath, funeral, house of keys, museum with those goddesses, Dedalus' song. Then that bawler in Barney Kiernan's. Got my own back there. Drunken ranters. What I said about his God made him wince. Mistake to hit back. Or? No. Ought to go home and laugh at themselves" (*U* 380). He lingers until nine o'clock, and the sounding of the hour mocks him with its repeated "*Cuckoo*" (*U* 382).

The night chapters that follow introduce many new depths of obscurity and complexity as the narrative methods reflect the murky darkness. In "Oxen of the Sun" Bloom has made his way to the National Maternity Hospital to inquire about Mina Purefoy, and as he joins the carousing medicals in the commons room, news of the birth of her ninth child reaches him. Joyce severely tightens the stylistics as he combines the slaughter of the sacred oxen by Odysseus's sailors, the offense against fertility, with the nine months of gestation and nine centuries of the changes in prose style in English literature, resulting in the single most opaque chapter in the novel. The mode of narration is passed over to various British writers from the tenth through the nineteenth centuries, so that the events in the hospital refectory are "interpreted" by a succession of "voices," each adding new dimensions, new attitudes, new peculiarities. The change in style from paragraph to paragraph on one hand displays James Joyce's virtuosity as a parodist, but on the other calls into question the validity of any single narrative perspective. As the medicals irreverently discuss birth and motherhood, overwhelmingly supporting methods of contraception, Stephen in his cups decries "those Godpossibled souls that we nightly impossibilise, which is the sin against the Holy Ghost, Very God, Lord and Giver of Life"

(*U* 389), although we may suspect that he is mourning the works of artistic creation that remain unborn through wasted time and energy. Bloom worries about Stephen, "for that he lived riotously with those wastrels and murdered his goods with whores" (*U* 391), a crime against creative fertility, while Lynch mockingly crowns Stephen, declaring that the laurel leaves "will adorn you more fitly when something more, and greatly more, than a capful of light odes can call your genius father" (*U* 415). Stephen, after all, arrogantly announced that "If I call them into life across the waters of Lethe will not the poor ghosts troop to my call? Who supposes it? I, Bous Stephanoumenos, bullockbefriending bard, am lord and giver of their life" (*U* 415). And to add to the mockery, Mulligan appears out of the rain, having attending George Moore's party (to which Stephen had not been invited) to pass out his newly printed card: "*Mr Malachi Mulligan, Fertiliser and Incubator*" (*U* 402).

After the elaborate mock-celebration of the birth the medicals and the hangers-on rush out to the nearest pub for final drinks before closing time. Noisy and rambunctious, their mingled shouts and cries present a travesty of the nine hundred years of the development of elegant prose style, a disintegration into all manner of colloquial and dialectal distortions of the spoken language. At Burke's pub Lenehan spots the drunken Bantam Lyons, whom he had dissuaded from following Bloom's inadvertent tip on Throwaway, and he gives up a chance for one last free drink to slink away before Lyons spots him:

'Tis, sure, What say? In the speakeasy. Tight. I shee you, shir. Bantam, two days teetee. Mowsing nowt but claretwine. Garn! Have a glint, do. Gum, I'm jiggered. . . . Had the winner today till I tipped him a dead cert. . . . Decamping. Must you go? Off to mammy. Stand by. Hide my blushes someone. All in if he spots me. Comeahome, our Bantam. Horryvar, mong vioo. (*U* 426)

Soon afterward they all decamp as the pub closes, most of them to chase the fire engines to a blaze, Stephen led by Lynch to the brothels of nighttown, and Bloom following at a discreet distance.

The closing scene of "Oxen of the Sun" is recorded in a melange of disembodied voices, displacing narration completely, and anticipating the Circe chapter that follows. For his "Circe" Joyce chose total reliance on the dramatic mode, a play within a novel that is by far the longest section of *Ulysses,* although narration as such reenters through the back door of fully developed stage directions. The midnight world of nighttown invites comparison with a Walpurgisnacht, a witches' sabbath of magical transformations and hallucinations. The darkened set at the end of "Oxen," with its broken bits of idiosyncratic conversation, is suddenly and strangely lighted in "Circe," beginning with the opening stage direction: *"The Mabbot street entrance of nighttown, before which stretches an uncobbled tramsiding set with skeleton tracks, red and green will-o'-the-wisps and danger signals"* (*U* 429). The alternating lights color everything, and children look like *"stunted men and women,"* until the change in lighting reveals them as children—except that one *"gnome"* is seen to be not a child, but a collector of *"rags and bones"* (*U* 430). In this phantasmagoria, where reality and fantasy coexist, all events are subject to skeptical scrutiny. The Cissy Caffrey who was with Gerty on the Sandymount beach now appears as the consort of a British soldier, Private Carr (in itself a possible "double life" of bourgeois girl by day and wild hoyden by night, but Edy Boardman *seems* to be there in nighttown as well, as are the sailor-suited Caffrey children). Stephen and Lynch wend their way through the streets to Bella Cohen's, and Bloom independently finds his way there as well. Stephen's panic-stricken vision of his dead mother leads him to smash the lightshade and run into the streets, where he runs afoul of Private Carr and is knocked unconscious. It is a solicitious Bloom who bends over him at the end of the scene, hoping to revive him and rescue him, but also seeing at that time a vision of his dead son Rudy, who would now be almost eleven years old: *"a figure appears slowly, a fairy boy of eleven, a*

*changeling, kidnapped, dressed in an Eton suit with glass
shoes and a little bronze helmet, holding a book in his hand"*
(*U* 609). The live Stephen and the imagined Rudy share the
Circean stage at the fade-out, a pairing of the real and the
imaginary that has characterized the entire chapter.

The area of unreality in "Circe" proves particularly
misleading, especially if the reader attempts to separate and
classify the real events as discretely different from the
hallucinations that presumably take place in the minds of
Stephen Dedalus and Leopold Bloom. Everything that has
taken place during the course of the day seems to be
recapitulated during this midnight hour, as thousands of items
of background material reappear as parts of the fantasy,
including Bloom's father, mother, and grandfather, and at least
in such instances it is safe to assume that he is imagining
them—or are they only fantasy versions of the actual parents?
In his imagination Bloom is elevated to exalted heights of
fame and fortune, only to be turned against and hunted,
humiliated, and persecuted. The drama of infinite possibilities
is played out in bizarre forms, and every facet of their
environment conspires against both Stephen and Bloom, as
their hopes and dreams of glory are momentarily realized and
their secret dreads fulfilled as well. But just as Odysseus rescued
his sailors from Circe's spell and had them transformed back
into their natural forms, so Bloom emerges unscathed from
nighttown, bringing Stephen out with him. As the Eumaeus
chapter opens, the escape has been effected, and "preparatory
to anything else Mr Bloom brushed off the greater bulk of the
shavings and handed Stephen the hat and ashplant and bucked
him up generally in orthodox Samaritan fashion, which he
very badly needed" (*U* 612-13). The return homeward is now
under way, but en route they stop off at a cabman's shelter for
coffee and rather one-sided conversation, since Stephen has
reverted to a grumpy silence for most of the chapter,
answering Bloom's inquiries rather perfunctorily. The chapter
has as its key figure an ablebodied seaman named W. B.
Murphy, an actual Odysseus of sorts, who spins exaggerated

yarns about his navigational voyages that make every aspect of
him open to question. The hostile mood in the cabman's
shelter is enough to cause Bloom once again to rescue Stephen
and lead him home, the two now joined in amicable
friendship. And the excessively long-winded and almost
endless sentences of the chapter, its pompous and circuitous
rhetoric mirroring the fatigue of the protagonists, add to the
confined atmosphere from which they emerge into the fresh
night air.

"Ithaca" represents a true homecoming, an intimacy and
cordiality between Bloom and Stephen that, although it falls
short of perfect rapport or even the establishment of a
permanent relationship, as Bloom would wish, nonetheless
achieves that quality that comes to stand for Bloom—
equilibrium. Yet the format of the chapter is coldly inquisitional,
a catechism of 309 questions and answers that pretends toward
total objectivity, so that neither questioner nor answerer exists
as a human entity. And an overwhelming collection of new
pieces of information present themselves at this late stage of
Ulysses as we peek into Bloom's bureau drawers, in some ways
a better repository than Bloom's thoughts (his father's suicide
note and Haggadah are there, as well as the insurance policy,
bank passbook, and Canadian government stock informing us
that despite his loss of jobs the prudent Bloom is indeed quite
solvent). The sources of information in "Ithaca" are somewhat
mysterious, yet the reader assumes that the thoughts and
conversations of Bloom and Stephen are still the basic
repositories, in addition to what actually transpires and what is
actually uncovered at 7 Eccles Street. But the answers that
provide information are only as valid as the source can possibly
be, and depend on the value of the questions themselves.
When the question "Did it flow?" is asked of the water in the
Bloom kitchen sink, the "Yes" (*U* 671) answer is supplemented
by an inundation of technical information concerning the
waterworks that could only have its origins in a textbook or
brochure. Yet a question that may well have been nagging
throughout the day, whether Bloom was aware of how close he

was to tipping the Throwaway victory and whether he felt any dismay at not having bet on the horse, now manages to get itself asked somewhat obliquely, and the answer must come from Bloom's own reactions:

> His mood?
> He had not risked, he did not expect, he had not been disappointed, he was satisfied.
> What satisfied him?
> To have sustained no positive loss. To have brought a positive gain to others. Light to the gentiles. (*U* 676)

This degree of "equilibrium" seems almost uncanny in any human being, but there are indeed complementary facets of fears and anxieties in Bloom as well, the prospects of an old age of "Poverty," "Mendicancy," "Destitution," and the "Nadir of misery: the aged impotent disfranchised ratesupported moribund lunatic pauper" (*U* 725). And the "imprint of a human form, male" apparent in his bed causes him to dredge up a list of every possible lover or admirer that Molly may ever have had (*U* 731), a list that tells us much more about the possibilities of his jealousy than of her infidelity. And the list soon fades as he works his way through "Envy, jealousy, abnegation" to "Equanimity" (*U* 732-33), so that there will never be anything in *Ulysses* that really approximates Odysseus's slaughter of the 108 suitors in his Ithaca palace.

Molly's reveries in "Penelope" suggest ways of killing off the suitors: "where does their great intelligence come in Id like to know," she asks of men in general, "grey matter they have it all in their tail if you ask me" (*U* 757-58). She runs through various "possible" men and dismisses all of them with derision, including Simon Dedalus and Ben Dollard and Lenehan and John Henry Menton, and even the actual suitor of the day, Hugh (Blazes) Boylan:

no thats no way for him has he no manners nor no refinement nor no nothing in his nature slapping us behind like that on my bottom because I didnt call him Hugh the ignoramus that doesnt know poetry from a cabbage thats what you get for not keeping them in their proper place. (*U* 776)

Her thoughts weave and unweave through eight long sentences comprising over twoscore pages, absent of punctuation and meandering freely as she attempts to fall back asleep, a pure reservoir of practical and fantastic ideas, of annoyance and delight, of sharp observations about people and fuzzy recollections of the past, of resoluteness and indecision, and of multiple contradictions, till sleep begins to claim her and she sinks into a revery that confuses having been kissed at fifteen under the Moorish Wall in Gibraltar by Mulvey and at eighteen on the Hill of Howth by Leopold Bloom—a retreat to a state of innocence and romance.

In the whirlpool of the woman's expansive thoughts *Ulysses* has its irresolute conclusion, although primarily an odyssey of a good man's wanderings through a vaguely hostile world, and a further portrait of the artist still as a young man, but at loose ends and perhaps at the cutting edge of decision. What potential exists for Stephen may depend on how he evaluates the experiences of his day and the extent to which the encounter with Bloom—far from providing him with a surrogate father that he obviously does not want—offers him an insight into a larger world that contains the materials of his future art. For the Bloom marriage, which readers have worried about endlessly, the events of the day apparently suggest more difficulties than solutions, but it is not in the events that resolutions lie: the strength of character revealed by both Molly Bloom and Leopold Bloom (reasonableness, equanimity, tolerance, humanity, humor) offers far greater possibilities than the mistaken notion that Bloom asked for (and may receive) breakfast in bed on the morning of 17 June 1904. Their marriage is obviously a sounder one than any others we have seen in Dublin, as we remember the Dedaluses, the Breens, the MacDowells, the M'Coys, Martin Cunningham with a drunken wife, and Jack Power with a wife and mistress—unless we are tempted by the portrait of the Purefoys with their nine children. *Ulysses,* despite all of its imaginative forays into exotic regions and the mysteries and ironies that it contains, remains a novel of ordinary bourgeois life at a certain time and in a certain place, just as the story of the Blooms and Stephen and assorted Dubliners nonetheless captures ramifications of a world scene in the throes of incredible adventures. Rather than a deflation of Homer's heroic world, *Ulysses* subsumes that world and its potentials, along with its cruelties and absurdities, within a contemporary and exceedingly human frame, finding multiple ways of telling and retelling an ordinary and extraordinary tale.

6

Between a Sleep and a Wake

Writing an Impossible Book

The seventeen years of composition of *Finnegans Wake* were conducted in Paris, in an environment of avant-garde enthusiasms and excesses for which Joyce served as a reluctant high priest, at once part of the constituent body of *transition* and other little magazines in which the as-yet-untitled Work in Progress appeared, and still quietly aloof from all manifestos and movements. With *Ulysses* both a *succès de scandale* and a *succès d' estime,* and his finances now in good condition, Joyce established himself in Paris and vacationed at various resorts during the twenties and thirties, while the pattern of constant changes of address continued as it had in Trieste and Zurich— as indeed it had in his father's residences in Dublin. Work on the work in progress was sporadic and desultory, delayed by numerous eye operations and worries about his daughter's deteriorating mental condition, and the idea of handing over the incomplete project to James Stephens (although hardly likely to have been a serious one) exemplifies the state of Joyce's life in those turbulent years. Begun in the year that Ireland was wrenching itself free from the British Empire and in the throes of wrenching itself apart, and as Mussolini's fascism established itself in Rome, the *Wake* was finally concluded, titled, and published on the verge of World War Two. Whether a Chapelizod pubkeeper's dream or an erotic history of humankind or a pub yarn endlessly woven through a plethora of pub yarns, tall tales, and multifaceted narratives, *Finnegans Wake* obliquely subsumes the political events of the years of its composition, folding them away within the multitudes of events from time immemorial.

The degree of innovation in the *Wake* is of course extraordinary, so much so that it remains the single most difficult text of the modernist period and is in a sense unreadable—and not necessarily termed so in a pejorative manner. The book challenges and changes our modes of reading, requiring on one hand the explicative methods employed for reading poetry, and on the other a suspension of disbelief that allows the reader to open and reopen constantly the possibilities and multiplicities of interpretation. Some sections were rewritten numerous times, each revision further elaborating and complicating the texture of the narrative; others in the later stages of composition emerged as thoroughly convoluted constructions ready to be fit into the completed pattern unchanged, as Joyce sought both to perfect a single unified work and to alter constantly the conditions of literary response with every segment of the text. Unlike *Ulysses* it was written completely out of sequence, in bits and pieces and fixed set pieces, all of which Joyce eventually sewed together under a title that he had kept secret, insisting that he had a schematic plan in mind throughout. Contradictions abound: at various times Joyce insisted that every facet of the work was scrupulously honed to fit perfectly in place (and he even gave a long explication of the ramifications of one section), and at others he claimed that it was all merely intended to make the reader laugh. Serious critical attention has been focused on the rule that nothing in *Finnegans Wake* is nonsense, yet it is probably equally true that it is all pure nonsense, subsuming and perpetually violating the limitations of prosaic "sense." Readers and critics have consistently attempted to "translate" Joyce's language back into what he called "wideawake"

language—with barely marginal success—and have dismissed
some aspects of his tampering with language as trivial when
something less than direct explication emerges from their
frustrated efforts.

Perfectly adequate sense, for example, can easily be obtained
from a phrase as obvious as "O'Neill saw Queen Molly's pants"
(*FW* 495.27-28), where the skeletal model is the heraldic
motto, "Honi soit qui mal y pense." Certain suggestions within
the context establish the phrase as a "motto," remind us of the
origin in British royal history ("Saxontannery"), and even
indicate that the language is Old French ("ffrenchllatin"). That
all of this may well be outside the narrative of *Finnegans Wake*
is a condition that the reader takes under advisement at any
juncture of the book, since numerous skeins weave into the
narrative context from various allusive sources. More directly,
perhaps, the implications of voyeurism and sexual enticement
are germane to one of the basic plot elements, that two
maidens in Phoenix Park either expose themselves to the
Chapelizod pubkeeper Earwicker or are observed by him
urinating (or various other modifications of such actions),
while three soldiers presumably look on. Within this sort of a
narrative frame the passage yields to exegesis, as we read:

both the legintimate lady performers of display unquestionable,
Elsebett and Marryetta Gunning, H_2O, by that noblesse of leechers at
his Saxontannery with motto in Wwalshe's ffrenchllatin: O'Neill saw
Queen Molly's pants: and much admired engraving, meaning
complet manly parts during alleged recent act of our chief mergey
margey magistrades, five itches above the kneecap, as required by
statues. (*FW* 495.24-31)

An alternate source is the Dublin coat of arms which shows
two classic women holding up their skirts (Dublin wit has it
that they are careful of rain puddles, but that also can be
extended to their own making of water), as well as three
crowns (the soldiers), and the city motto. Extensive
investigation, then, can unearth many allusions and parallels
for a satisfactory "reading" of the passage, yet cannot explain
away the irrelevance of O'Neill and Molly: Gaelic rebel

chieftains and the heroine of *Ulysses* can be called in to serve, but one senses that it is only the "accident" of similar sounds that results in their otherwise meaningless presence. To an upholder of the efficacy of the motto of the Knights of the Garter, O'Neill saw Queen Molly's pants is a travesty; to those who find *Honi soit qui mal y pense* somewhat silly, Joyce's version is comparably silly. Literal "translation" may have less significance in reading the motto than a sense of the play between the original and the variant, and a sense of the nature of parody operative in *Finnegans Wake*.

On every page dozens of names, titles, mottoes, and quotations leap into double focus, the original and the variant vying with each other for privileged attention. How the reader determines the relationship between the two can alter the method of reading and of perception. The phrase "was Parish worth thette mess" (*FW* 199.8-9) can either glide by un-observed or can immediately encounter its original in *"Paris vaut bien une messe,"* Henri IV's justification for conversion to Roman Catholicism in order to assume the French throne. The "locale" of the reference is the city bisected by a river, so Paris has its rational place, along with Dublin and London and Budapest ("the tits of buddy and the loits of pest and to peer was Parish worth thette mess" [*FW* 199.7-9]) in a chapter inundated with hundreds of rivers. The previous chapter had done a great deal to establish Shem the Penman as a character in the *Wake* who had abandoned his native Dublin to live and debauch and write his book in Paris, so the phrase has legitimate contextual associations, while Joyce biography places the author as well within a similar context (Joyce had commissioned Herbert Gorman to write and publish a biography of him which then serves as another "pre-text" for the phrase). The *Honi soit* allusion has one direct variant in "Honeys wore camelia paints" (*FW* 113.17), where again, although fruit and birds and flowers are operative within the context, the punning words appear wholly arbitrary, whereas variants on Paris-is-well-worth-a-Mass (or Joyce's version of it) have rather oblique echoes elsewhere in *Finnegans Wake*:

"Was life worth leaving? Nej!" (*FW* 230.25) locates the Shem exile back along the banks of the Liffey in Dublin, but also implies the existential question whether life is worth living (the apparent negative, *Nej!*, is undercut by being a positive in Greek). For Henry of Navarre the statement is a strong assertion, which Joyce in the *Parish* version makes into a weak conditional and in the *liffe* version definitely interrogative. It is a pathetical interrogative when Shem's sister Issy asks, "Is love worse living?" (*FW* 269.n1), but had its assertive potency in an earlier "that's what makes lifework leaving and the world's a cell for citters to cit in" (*FW* 12.1-2). The full panoply of possibilities ranges widely and indecisevly, if one insists on decisiveness from *Finnegans Wake*. Despite the clarity of the allusion, all possibilities remain open, perhaps all the more so since a hint of the Paris of Troy who caused quite another kind of mess may lurk not too far from the surface.

Efforts to extract "meanings" from *Finnegans Wake* have had only marginal success during the years since its publication, perhaps because Joyce's language allows for greater accumulations of meaning than a definite narrowing into an accepted concept that precludes others, and in many cases the accumulations contain inherent contradictions. Joyce has variously indicated that Molly's "yes" at the conclusion of *Ulysses* was the strong avowal of affirmation as well as the feminine submissive, two concepts that invite conflict, while the concluding "the" of the *Wake,* which he maintained was the weakest word in the English language, nonetheless retains the root word for God in Greek. The fusion of opposites has been assumed as a purposeful thematic statement in the *Wake,* Joyce's nod to the theories of Giordano Bruno, yet can we actually find consistent and definite synthesis in the text, or a complication and diversification of oppositions developing from fused antagonisms? The artificial joining of the opening and closing sentence fragments of the book has become a critical commonplace in *Wake* analysis, but a close examination of the fusion indicates that the join does not quite hold. The *Wake* begins in the middle of a sentence and ends with a series of dependent participles to a sentence which never materializes, and the "joining" produces what is *almost* a sentence:

A way a lone a last a loved a long the (*FW* 628.15-16) riverrun, past Eve and Adam's, from swerve of shore to bend of bay, brings us by a commodius vicus of recirculation back to Howth Castle and Environs. (*FW* 3.1-3)

The best will in the world will not accurately join what has never actually been severed: the syntax is faulty and the mood of the two sections incompatible—yet a sense that these two pieces move toward each other almost inevitably remains. The fragments tunnel at each other from opposite sides in the dark, to meet but not quite join, a condition that persists throughout Joyce's "night book." *Finnegans Wake* frequently titles itself, and two corresponding examples are *"The Suspended Sentence"* (*FW* 106.13-14) and "the book of Doublends Jined" (*FW* 20.15-16).

Joyce has been credited with (and accused of) destroying the English language, the language of the British conquerors of Ireland, and rebelling against everything bourgeois, even the esteemed language system, but Joyce himself claimed that what he destroyed in the writing of *Finnegans Wake* he also reconstructed, and the net result is the creation of a language, what he called night language, but what commentators on occasion insist on referring to as dream language. From the closing section of "Oxen of the Sun" through the four succeeding chapters, various night languages were developed stylistically in *Ulysses* to contain the night world, and for the *Wake* a new night language (encompassing multiple variants) takes precedence. Joyce explained that he was turning his back on "wideawake" day language, adding that he was also abandoning its "cutanddry grammar." Literal grammarians can undoubtedly diagram many a *Wake* sentence, but many others defy artificial structuring, although the long, overly extended, and complex "sentences" often give the impression of having a syntactical flow. Night language always "approximates" actual apprehension, a sense of an operative reality, a movement toward conceptualization and confinement, but always eludes the actual, the definite, the defined.

The first word of the text can be allowed to serve as a paradigm of the linguistic conditions of *Finnegans Wake:* *riverrun* has readily been accepted as a poetic neologism somehow compounding river and running (flowing) to suggest the River Liffey in Dublin flowing past Adam and Eve's Church, and metaphorically the river of time running past our primal parents toward the present. The juncture of the noun acting actively with the verb form adds to the potency of the compound, an effect that is lost if the definite article at the end of the book is allowed to interfere with *riverrun.* The word also suggests "reverend," especially when an Irish intonation is introduced, and the relationship of a Reverend Father with Adam and Eve's Church satisfies a kind of associative logic that readers quickly assume as operative in the *Wake.* If read as a salutation, Reverend becomes the beginning of a letter, the person addressed, and all of *Finnegans Wake* an enormous epistolary text containing within its frame numerous other missives, although the placement of the word Reverend within the assumed syntax of the "sentence" puts it out of kilter entirely, suggesting the effect instead of a palimpsest, the letter read "through" the narrative text of the running river.

Intimations of such an epistle and the honorific form of address are apparent throughout the *Wake,* or become apparent through accumulation. A very early version seems to be missing its salutation, but contains a cryptic reference to "muchears and midgers and maggets" (*FW* 11.25), while a later one makes an attempt at locating an addressee: "Dear whom it proceded to mention Maggy's well & allathome's health well" (*FW* 111.10-11), with further elaborations extending to "Maggy's tea or your majesty" (*FW* 116.24). Finally, Anna Livia's letter has its implicit notation, as it expands the possibilities while being relatively specific: "Dear. And we go on to Dirtdump. Reverend. May we add majesty?"

(*FW* 615.12-13). The pieces take shape as in a kaleidoscopic mosaic: Maggy may well be the writer or recipient of a letter, or the Maggies may well be cousins across the seas and imply both the writer and recipient, but on another level and more expanded scale a revered and majestic personage—king, father, priest, or God—is addressed, although not without a corresponding deflation (husband) as Dear Dirty Dublin. In the opening of the chapter that both is and contains Anna Livia's "untitled mamafesta memorialising the Mosthighest" (untitled, hence unaddressed), the Paternoster is parodied as "haloed be her eve, her singtime sung, her rill be run, unhemmed as it is uneven" (*FW* 104.1-4), *rill be run* as both the riverrun of the Anna Liffey and the addressed Reverend. The two readings of *riverrun* are neither mutually exclusive nor perfectly fused, nor does either one or a compound of the two necessarily close out other possibilities (the French *riverain* is highly suggestive). The flexibility of the night language of the *Wake* circumvents fixed closures, while the precision of that language disallows unlicensed free associations of meanings and interpretations.

Just as early evaluations of *Ulysses* focused on its chaotic randomness, despite the highly schematized structures now apparent, so *Finnegans Wake* appears to be an uncharted minefield. The sense of a structure depends on the division into four books, the first consisting of eight chapters, while the second and third have four each, the final one a single chapter ending in incompletion. Joyce indicated that the four-part structure was intentional and implicated Giambattista Vico's cycles of history as germane to the pattern, but warned not to take Vico's role in the *Wake* too seriously (although he admits to using Vico "for all he was worth"). Book 1 then is viewed as corresponding to a theocratic age (The Book of the Parents), book 2 to a heroic age (The Book of the Sons), and book 3 as the democratic age (The Book of the People), with book four as a Recorso. The pattern holds up only marginally well: indeed the first four chapters seem to introduce an arriving hero in Humphrey Chimpden Earwicker, displacing vaguer heroic figures from a prehistoric past, who settles down, raises a family, and at a certain time in the recent past has committed an indiscretion that has volatile repercussions. The next four chapters apparently recapitulate these "events," but already in terms of his wife, Anna Livia Plurabelle, and his children, twin sons Shaun and Shem, and younger daughter Issy. Book 2 situates a particular evening during which the now much younger children are at play and at their lessons before going to bed, and the pubkeeper Earwicker is in his bar with his customers, gets drunk and passes out, eventually finding his way to bed. Book 3 carries through the night, Earwicker's drunken dream reactivating his feelings of guilt, until an early morning scene reveals the parents in bed disturbed by an awakened child—time having reverted to the early marriage days of the parents. Book 4 suggests a real dawn breaking on Chapelizod, and the flowing into Dublin Bay of the Liffey.

No plot summary of *Finnegans Wake*, no matter how concise or how elaborately extensive, can capture the narrative condition in which there is no single narrative. On one hand the digressions and interruptions return to the basic plot of one family of five, plus two servants of sorts (vaguely grandparent figures), and a dozen customers that may well include four old men; yet on the other hand the tale of Earwicker misbehaving with two girls in the park, overseen by three soldiers who spread the tale until a "Cad" accosts Earwicker in the same park and manages some sort of accusation, never gets told despite the six-hundred-odd pages of *Wake* narration. All other tales participate in and diverge from the hint of a central narrative, and the multiplicity of characters with numerous tales to tell (on or off the subject) contribute to an oral history of the world, filtered through a universal language attempting to duplicate the nonverbal qualities of the world of dreams. The shift that Joyce had made from the narrative method of *Stephen Hero* to *A Portrait* was a shift from linear progression to a small series of compartmentalized packages of discrete units, each containing a particular construction of smaller units, a method elaborated upon in *Ulysses* and perfected in *Finnegans Wake*. Rather than a continuous narrative, the *Wake* consists of packets of linked, blended, and interrupted tales (some no more complete than a single phrase) and a mélange of voices performing narrational services independent of any central intention. Not only does the book contain multitudes, but these multitudes interact and interconnect at junctures determined by accidental and coincidental factors, the net result of which is an almost seamless garment that the chapter separations only minimally affect. The four-part structuring implied by the segregation into "books" is both corroborated and belied by an "unseen" structuring that runs parallel with the more obvious one: instances of silence that serve as caesuras to the narratives and as bridges between them. Early in the first chapter the word appears alone and centered on a line:

(Silent.) (*FW* 14.6)

Toward the end of the fourth chapter it appears within a sentence set off by colons (":silence:" [*FW* 98.2]), and in the middle of the eleventh chapter (book 2, chapter 3) it is again centered on a line of its own:

(Silents) (*FW* 334.31)

And in book 3, chapter 3 (the fifteenth chapter), it recurs as:

SILENCE. (*FW* 501.7)

with white space above and below as well. No two of the four are the same (*Silent, silence, Silents, SILENCE*), reflecting the narrative circumstances of the *Wake*, where no two narratives are the same, and no one narrative the same as it is being told and retold.

The easy conclusion that "*Finnegans Wake* is a Dream" does not account for the multiple discontinuities that not only disrupt but give coherence to the narrative structures of the text—dreams are invariably overdetermined in their continuities, quite unlike the *Wake*. Nor does "dream language" explain the interlaced structures, for those few portions that are quite consciously (and literarily) dreamlike are quite conventional in the depiction in language of the visual contents of dreams, as when Earwicker is "recording" his dream vision of his favored son, Shaun the Post:

And as I was jogging along in a dream as dozing I was was dawdling, arrah, methought broadtone was heard and the creepers and the gliders and flivvers of the earth breath and the dancetongues of the woodfires and the hummers in their ground all vociferated echoating: Shaun! Shaun! Post the post! with a high voice and O, the higher on high the deeper and low, I heard him so! And lo, mescemed somewhat came of the noise and somewho might amove allmurk. Now, 'twas as clump, now mayhap. When look, was light and now 'twas as flasher, now moren as the glaow. Ah, in unlitness 'twas in very similitude, bless me, 'twas his belted lamp! Whom we dreamt was a shaddo, sure, he's lightseyes, the laddo! (*FW* 404.3-24)

There is hardly a gram of psychological dream content in this dreamologue; instead, there is pure spook-invoking, a fairly wideawake narration in which Earwicker conjures up an image from a darkened landscape full of strange sounds and noises. It is characteristic of the *Wake* that all functioning variations and alterations of expected narrational techniques are viable within its cosmos, and merely one more twist that the invocation of a dream should result in language of least similitude to traditional assumptions about dreams.

Reading *Finnegans Wake* has been likened to collecting sand in a sieve, and experienced readers of the book have learned to read selectively, searching for specific threads or clusters at each reading. Some have persistently attempted to read the "plot" of the *Wake* and establish a chronology for the Earwicker (or Porter, on a literal level) family situation that straightens out the time warps of Joyce's method of presentation, obtain cameo descriptions of the principal characters, and determine the events of the Earwicker indiscretion and its reverberations. Others have sought the major themes they find surfacing throughout: the endurance and flexibility of humankind, the comic foibles of human pretensions, the absurdity of feelings of guilt in a fallible universe, the monumental achievement of the building of cities or (conversely) the futility of man's accomplishments in the face of the relentless permanence of nature, the vying of brothers for rights of succession, the supplanting of fathers by sons, the woman as temptress, provoker of violence, healer and bringer of peace, the rivalry of mothers and nubile daughters, the eternal presence of man and woman in the natural landscape as mountain and river. Occasionally a reader decides that *Finnegans Wake* has a central theme or a dominant message, that it is essentially about Shakespeare or Kierkegaard or the Easter Passion or the Irish Civil War or *The Book of the Dead* or "The Ballad of Tim Finnegan": each of these tends to narrow the focus of an otherwise expansive universe contained in the *Wake,* yet any effort to capture that expansiveness can result in the loss of too many grains of sand.

Finnegans Wake constantly gives the impression of a rhythmic flow of infinite variation, of stylistic changes from section to section, from paragraph to paragraph, and even within individual sentences, and of areas of increased density and murkiness, relieved by pockets of near-lucidity—as when the text addresses the reader directly and urgently: "Now, patience; and remember patience is the great thing, and above all things else we must avoid anything like being or becoming out of patience" (*FW* 108.8-10). Such messages in the *Wake* are invariably "signed" and substantiated, undergirded by existing authority, and the call for patience suggests philosophic thought (Confucius) or historical example (Robert Bruce and the spider): "master Kung's doctrine of the meang" and "brothers Bruce with whom are incorporated their Scotch spider" (*FW* 108.11-12, 14-15). At other instances the text proves rather insulting to the reader (or to some other reader, either inside or outside the text): "(Stoop) if you are abcedminded, to this claybook, what curios of signs (please stoop), in this allaphbed! Can you rede (since We and Thou had it out already) its world?" (*FW* 18.16-18). Or, conversely (or even conjunctively) an intrusive reader quarrels with the manner of presentation, demanding simplification or even cessation. *Finnegans Wake* sets up a dialogue between a vast host of respondents and correspondents, not least of which is a contingent of readers. When the "please stoop" request is heard again, a different voice with a different tone addresses a different audience:

Dark ages clasp the daisy roots, Stop, if you are a sally of the allies, hot off Minnowaurs and naval actiums, picked engagements and banks of rowers. Please stop if you're a B.C. minding missy, please do. But should you prefer A.D. stepplease. And if you miss with a venture it serves you girly well glad. (*FW* 272.9-15)

At all times in the *Wake* the immediate contexts determine innumerable changes in existing conditions—in tone and in texture, and in the relation of component parts to each other.

The Characters in the Drama, the Caricatures in the Dream

Most "interpretations" of the *Wake* are predictably based on the handful of lucid moments when the miasma momentarily clears and one encounters tangible and definable elements. Each of the *Wake* personages, for example, can be noticed and examined on occasion—as the picture of Shaun in his Royal Mail Delivery uniform has demonstrated in his father's dream imagination. Elsewhere he is seen in double-focus as the Chuff of the pantomime played by an actor (triple-focus if we assume that he is a child playacting the role of the adult actor): "CHUFF (Mr Sean O'Mailey, see the chalk and sanguine pictograph on the safety drop), the fine frank fairheaded fellow of the fairytales" (*FW* 220.11-13), and still elsewhere as an infant, "nicechild Kevin Mary (who was going to be commandeering chief of the choirboys' brigade the moment he grew up under all the auspices) irishsmiled in his milky way of cream dwibble and onage tustard and dessed tabbage" (*FW* 555.16-19). From these and similar approximations and intimations the reader builds up a portrait and a story line (none of it necessarily accurate at all instances) of the good brother, angelic as a child and solid as an adult, his goodness

shot through with cloying self-righteousness and probably
hypocrisy, a deliverer of the written word but presumably not
capable of writing the message, a uniformed upholder of the
tenets of society as choirboy and cleric, postman and policeman,
soldier and solid citizen (the Irish tricolor seen in the color of
the foods he eats as an infant). Readers have either seen
Kevin-Chuff-Shaun as the villain of the piece, the target of
Joyce's bohemian prejudices, or as the corresponding half of
the balanced brothers, the Yang to Shem's Yin. He has often
been viewed as a composite of Joyce's "antagonists," of Joycean
alter egos: his brother Stanislaus, John McCormack, Eamon de
Valera, Wyndham Lewis, T.S. Eliot, Oliver St. John Gogarty, et
al—especially if one reads the *Wake* as extended autobiography.

By contrast with the bourgeois brother the portrait of the
dissolute Shem the Penman is one of highly developed
caricature. As infant he is already "badbrat Jerry Godolphing
(who was hurrying to be cardinal scullion in a night refuge as
bald as he was cured enough unerr all the hospitals)
furrinfrowned down his wrinkly waste of methylated spirits,
ick, and lemoncholy lees, ick, and pulverised rhubarbarorum,
icky" (*FW* 555.20-24). At the earliest the child foreshadows
the adult, the "tragic jester" who "sobbed himself
wheywhingingly sick of life on some sort of rhubarbarous
maundarin yellagreen funkleblue windigut diodying applejack
squeezed from sour grapefruice" (*FW* 171.15-18). As
participant in the Mime he is "GLUGG (Mr Seumas
McQuillad, hear the riddles between the robot in his dress
circular and the gagster in the rogues' gallery), the bold bad
bleak boy of the storybooks, who, when the tabs go up, as we
discover, because he knew to mutch, has been divorced into
disgrace" (*FW* 219.22-220.2), debauched drunkard, lascivious
betrayer, and writer of riddles.

Shem has an entire chapter devoted to him (the seventh),
unlike Shaun, but one can assume that Shaun's talents are oral
rather than literary, and his is indeed the voice that narrates
the chapter about his brother. As the scribe Shem may be
writing at his mother's dictation and is her favorite son,

her entire Mamafesta chapter is signed by him at the end, "Shem the Penman" (*FW* 125.23). The Penman chapter begins with a clear enough nominal association with James Joyce himself ("Shem is as short for Shemus as Jem is joky for Jacob" [*FW* 169.1]), and contains a portrait that verges on the cubistic but nonetheless has autobiographic characteristics:

Shem's bodily getup, it seems, included an adze of a skull, an eight of a larkseye, the whoel of a nose, one numb arm up a sleeve, fortytwo hairs off his uncrown, eighteen to his mock lip, a trio of barbels from his megageg chin (sowman's son), the wrong shoulder higher than the right, all ears, an artificial tongue with a natural curl, not a foot to stand on, a handful of thumbs, a blind stomach, a deaf heart, a loose liver, two fifths of two buttocks, one gleetsteen avoirdupoider for him, a manroot of all evil, a salmonkelt's thinskin, eelsblood in his cold toes, a bladder tristended. (*FW* 169.11-20)

All of the traits displayed, his cosmopolitanism, his intemperance and lechery, his cowardice and lack of patriotism (and Shaun makes the most of all of these), give way to the essence of his role as literary artist: "he scrabbled and scratched and scriobbled and skrevened nameless shamelessness about everybody ever he met" and "used to stipple endlessly inartistic portraits of himself" (*FW* 182.13-14, 18-19). He certainly is the author of all of Joyce's previous work, especially "his usylessly unreadable Blue Book of Eccles, *è de tènèbres*" (*FW* 179.26-27), as well as the Bible and the plays of Shakespeare (and perhaps all of literature), and is at present at work "writing the mystery of himself in furniture" (*FW* 184.9-10), so that *Finnegans Wake* is now in progress, being written and rewritten by Shem. To do so he makes his own indelible ink from his own excrement, using an alchemical formula through psalmic incantation in order to write "over every square inch of the only foolscap available, his own body" (*FW* 185.35-36).

The brother battle has ramifications throughout the *Wake* and is never far from the surface at any time in the evolving of the numerous circumstances. On one level it replicates the encounter of Earwicker and the Cad in the park, as each generation reenacts the history of the previous one with a difference: as children Chuff and Glugg fight for preference, as schoolboys Kev and Dolph quarrel over their homework (in each case the "object" is the sister and the mother), and as young adults Kevin and Jerry both claim possession of the all-important document (the letter, the manifesto, the text), and seek to usurp the position of the father. The initial brother rivalry of Cain and Abel contests the cosmopolitan with the man of nature, and indeed Shem "preferred Gibsen's teatime salmon tinned . . . to the plumpest roeheavy lax" (*FW* 170.26-28), and the later juxtaposition of Jacob and Esau allows them to squabble over the patrimony. (If there is a specific Ur-text for *Finnegans Wake,* comparable to Homer's *Odyssey* for *Ulysses,* it is most probably the Book of Genesis.) And even such brotherly companionships as those of David and Jonathan, Castor and Pollux, Roland and Oliver, and Achilles and Patroclus are perverted in the *Wake* into fractious antagonisms, behind which lurks the epic battle of Lucifer and the archangel Michael ("All Saints beat Belial! Mickil Goals to Nichil!" [*FW* 175.5]), a depiction of which is contained in a mezzotint over the Earwicker bed.

The War in Heaven prefigures all the wars conducted by the nations of the earth, and many of them in the *Wake* are eponymously designated by contending generals, particularly Napoleon and Wellington. The Phoenix Park in the western edge of Dublin, adjoining Chapelizod, houses a Wellington monument and is the scene of both Earwicker's sin (analogous to Adam's transgression in the Garden of Eden) and his confrontation with the cad with a pipe (the celestial skirmish), and serves as the fields of Waterloo, especially since the Earwicker-and-the-Two-Girls involved urination, either his observed by them or theirs by him: "Hence when the clouds roll by, jamey, a proudseye view is enjoyable of our mounding's mass, now Wallinstone national museum, with, in some greenish distance, the charmful waterloose country and the two quitewhite villagettes who hear show of themselves so gigglesome minxt the follyages, the prettilees!" (*FW* 7.36-8.4). A particularly archetypal war, also involving the British and including Irish soldiery, is the Crimean War (the word containing "crime"), celebrated in literature by Tennyson's "Charge of the Light Brigade" ("plunders to night of you, blunders what's left of you" [*FW* 188.12]), and involving English generals who have left their names to articles of clothing—the kind of absurdity that Joyce considered applicable to his comic treatment of world history: "He was enmivallupped. Chromean fastion. With all his cannonball wappents. In his raglanrock and his malakoiffed bulbsbyg and his varnashed roscians and his cardigans blousejagged and his scarlett manchokuffs and his treecoloured camiflag and his perikopendolous gaelstorms" (*FW* 339.9-13)—seven articles of clothing are paramount in the *Wake* as epic investiture. The Crimean War, and particularly the Battle of Sevastopal ("Sea vaast a pool!" [*FW* 338.14]), are reduced to a pub tale presumably narrated by John Stanislaus Joyce of "How Buckley Shot the Russian General": "How Burghley shuck the rackushant Germanon. For Ehren, boys, gobrawl!" (*FW* 338.2-3).

Woven into the fabric of *Finnegans Wake* is a history of British imperial wars, as casually catalogued in oblique ways by an Irish comic perspective. The visit to the "Willingdone Museyroom" is the major focus on the Napoleonic war as cobwebbed history, the history of dusty souvenirs and memorabilia, in which the Dublin-born Duke of Wellington finds himself at "Waterloose" confronted by three Napoleons and a pair of "jinnies," an enactment of Earwicker's indiscretion in Phoenix Park: "This is the crimealine of the alps hooping to sheltershock the three lipoleums. This is the jinnies with their legahorns feinting to read in their handmade's book of stralegy while making their war undisides the Willingdone. The jinnies is a cooin her hand and the jinnies is a ravin her hair and the Willingdone git the band up" (*FW* 8.29-34). The Battle of Sevastopal is recreated in a television skit in which Shaun and Shem take roles as Butt and Taff to narrate and recreate the campaign (which for a while becomes a horse race, but most often is reduced to the shooting of the Russian

General while he is defecating by the Irish Captain Buckley, insulted when turf is used as toilet tissue):

In the heliotropical noughttime following a fade of transformed Tuff and, pending its viseversion, a metenergic reglow of beaming Batt, the bairdboard bombardment screen, if tastefully taut guraniam satin, tends to teleframe and step up to the charge of the light barricade. Down the photoslope in syncopanc pulses, with the bitts bugtwug their teffs, the missledhropes, glitteraglatteraglutt, borne by their carnier walve. Spraygun rakes and splits them from a double focus: grenadite, damnymite, alextronite, nichilite: and the scanning firespot of the sgunners traverses the rutilanced illustred sunksundered lines. Shlossh! A gaspel truce leaks out over the caeseine coatings. Amid a fluorescence of spectracular mephiticism there caoculates through the inconoscope steadily a still, the figure of a fellowchap in the wohly ghast, Popey O'Donoshough, the jesuneral of the russuates. (FW 349.6-15)

Reduction to comic absurdity succeeds as the operative method throughout the handling of historical material in *Finnegans Wake,* and the war motif is brought closer to home with the Great War of 1914 and the Easter Rising of 1916, both of which Shem avoids in his Swiss refuge ("he collapsed carefully under a bedtick from Schwitzer's" [*FW* 176.34-35]). The two conflicts are collapsed together and represented by their constituent colors and passed off as a sporting event, "the grand germogall allstar bout was harrily the rage between our weltingtoms extraordinary and our pettythicks the mar-shalaisy and Irish eyes of welcome were smiling daggers down their backs, when the roth, vice and blause met the noyr blank and rogues and the grim white and cold bet the black fighting tans" (*FW* 176.19-25). In the thick of these interlocked conflicts, extended to include the Troubles in Ireland with the British Black and Tans, and to dip back into the previous century for Wellington, Joyce's personal concerns creep in with determination: *Ulysses* had been suppressed in America by the bluestockinged Vice League and illegally pirated by Samuel Roth, hence the colors of the United States flag as *roth, vice and blause.* The sublime and the ridiculous, the exalted and the debased, the macrocosmic and its microcosmic reflection are juxtaposed in constant alliance, so that the history of the individual (Joyce himself or Shem or Earwicker) contains the historic development of the human race. Yet, though the scene is often Phoenix Park ("the wide expanse of our greatest park" [*FW* 35.7-8]), the Earwickers' kitchen midden and the Garden of Eden, the notorious Phoenix Park Murders of 1882, hidden in the landscape ("O foenix culprit!" [*FW* 23.16]), are carefully kept from view.

The sister Isabel/Issy is a far more shadowy figure than her two highly prevalent brothers, and perhaps the most enigmatic "character" in the *Wake*. Her "origins" have been traced to a Christine Beauchamps, a patient of the American neurologist Morton Prince, whose study of the case, *The Dissociation of a Personality*, provides a psychological base for Issy as the mirror girl ("best from cinder Christinette if prints chumming" [*FW* 280.21-22]), although the more literary "pre-texts" by Lewis Carroll, *Alice in Wonderland* and *Through the Looking-Glass*, have even stronger affinities with the capricious Issy ("Alicious, twinstreams, twinestraines, through alluring glass or alas in jumboland?" [*FW* 528.17-18]), especially since Joyce was aware that Lewis Carroll had shifted his interest from Alice Liddell to a younger girl, Isa Bowman, who portrayed Alice on stage. The suggestion that Earwicker harbors lecherous intentions toward young girls (*two* young girls, as witness the incident in the park) provides the motif of sexual guilt, especially if the girl is his own daughter. (The dream censor, however, intervenes and changes daughter to a more remote relative: "two cozes from Niece" [*FW* 608.7-8]). Incest is never far from home in this tightly intrafamiliar narrative, as all combinations of possibilities are entertained, at times with uncomfortable intensity, but most often playfully and even mockingly. After all, the dreaming father of a grown daughter might accidentally substitute the image of the young girl he had married many years ago for the young daughter who resembles her. Anna Livia when he first met her was "just a young thin pale soft shy slim slip of a thing then" (*FW*

202.27), and she remembers herself in comparison to Issy: "Just a whisk brisk sly spry spink spank sprint of a thing theresomere" (*FW* 627.4-5). The horror of sexual guilt may fade away once the time perspective shifts the focus from the present to the past, and in the *Wake* past, present, and future are always in a state of flux: "Anna was, Livia is, Plurabelle's to be" (*FW* 215.24).

In Book 3, chapter 4, where the children are infants at dawn in their cots, Issy is romantically described through the backward movement of time, bringing her from a twenty-year-old back to infancy in regressive stages, each cloyingly saccharine, as a pastiche of sentimental literature that Joyce employed in the Nausicaa chapter of *Ulysses:*

night by silentsailing night while infantina Isobel (who will be blushing all day to be, when she growed up one Sunday, Saint Holy and Saint Ivory, when she took the veil, the beautiful presentation nun, so barely twenty, in her pure coif, sister Isobel, and next Sunday, Mistlemas, when she looked a peach, the beautiful Samaritan, still as beautiful and still in her teens, nurse Saintette Isabelle, with stiffstarched cuffs but on Holiday, Christmas, Easter mornings when she wore a wreath, the wonderful widow of eighteen springs, Madame Isa Veuve La Belle, so sad but lucksome in her boyblue's long black with orange blossoming weeper's veil) for she was the only girl they loved, as she is the queenly pearl you prize, because of the way the night that first we met she is bound to be, methinks, and not in vain, the darling of my heart, sleeping in her april cot. (*FW* 556.1-14)

Not yet designated as the object of her aging father's lust, she is nonetheless the apple of her brothers' eyes, *the only girl they loved,* and consequently the cause of dissension and rivalry between them. As boys they squabble over her, play games with her as the prize, and as men they fight chivalric duels and engage in global warfare.

As Nuvoletta the nubile Issy saucily tempts the two vying antagonists, the Mookse and the Gripes, but to no avail, since one is blind and the other deaf, and both are obviously clerics, probably even pontiffs. So, since neither she nor "her feignt reflection, Nuvoluccia" (*FW* 157.24) succeeds, she resigns herself to the realization that it is all merely love's labors lost ("mild's vapour moist" [*FW* 157.23]), and disappears. As Margareena she is involved with a pair of Romans, Burrus and Caseous, and apparently unable to choose between them ("Margareena she's very fond of Burrus, but, alick and alack!, she velly fond of chee" [*FW* 166.30-31]), she resolves the dilemma by abandoning both in favor of a third: "A cleopatrician in her own right she at once complicates the position while Burrus and Caseous are contending for her misstery by implicating herself with an elusive Antonius, a wop who would appear to hug a personal interest in refined chees of all chades at the same time as he wags an antomine art of being rude like the boor" (*FW* 166.34-167.3). The Nuvoletta version remains fairly innocent, the Margareena scenario somewhat less so; and when a licentious film depicts "an old geeser who calls on his skirt," she is a vamp who gets "tolloll Mr Hunker" to buy her expensive clothes, only to dash off with "Arty, Bert or possibly Charley Chance." The plot has reverted to the Old Man and the Young Girl (Joyce mined the newspapers for this one, a scandalous court trial in which the story of "Daddy" Browning and his chorus girl, "Peaches," caused a sensation), a plot that has its twist when we learn that

old grum he's not so clean dippy between sweet you and yum (not on your life, boy! not in those trousers! not by a large jugful!) for someplace on the sly, where Furphy he isn't by, old grum has his gel number two (bravewow, our Grum!) and he would like to canoodle her too some part of the time for he is downright fond of his number one but O he's fair mashed on peaches number two so that if he could only canoodle the two, chivee chivoo, all three would feel genuinely happy, it's as simple as A. B. C., the two mixers, we mean, with their cherrybum chappy (for he is simply shamming dippy) if they all were afloat in a dreamlifeboat, hugging two by two in his zoo-do-you-do, a tofftoff for thee, missymissy for me and howcameyou-e'enso for Farber, in his tippy, upindown dippy, tiptoptippy canoodle, can you? Finny. (*FW* 65.5-33)

The "geeser" has his two "gels," and Peaches Number One at least has her three A.B.C. swains, so as the camera moves back from the depiction of the Old Man and his Young Girl, it discloses the Park incident of Earwicker, the two maidens, and the three soldiers—the basic sexual misadventure of *Finnegans Wake*.

Uncovering Browning and his Peaches in the daily press corroborated for Joyce the active, present-day recapitulation of a classic situation, and he inculpated various older gentlemen with often underaged girls—and preferably a pair of girls. To Lewis Carroll and his Alice and Isa he added Jonathan Swift and his Stella and Vanessa; they are a pair of saucy sisters with an anagrammatic Jonathan in "all's fair in vanessy, were sosie sesthers wroth with twone nathandjoe" (*FW* 3.11-12), since both women were named Esther ("from Yesthers late Yhesthers. . . . Astale of astoun. Grand owld marauder!" [*FW* 624.25-25), and equally addicted to vanity: "swift and still a vain essaying!" (*FW* 486.26-27). Swift's *A Tale of a Tub* (*Astale of astoun*) involved the three religions of Peter, Jack, and Martin, who then provide the three soldiers as well as the two maidens: "her issavan and essavans and her patter-jackmartins about all them inns and ouses. Tilling a teel of a tum" (7.4-5).

Issy and her mirror image suggest personal vanity as well as the more extreme split personality that Morton Prince found in Christine Beauchamps and in her evil other self, Sally, and Dr. Prince relates the attempts of his patient to seduce him. Joyce, therefore, involves the doctor as another "old man" with a young girl, as Issy moons over "My prince of the courts who'll beat me to love," adding, "but don't tell him or I'll be the mort of him!" (*FW* 460.12-13, 22). Joyce's daughter Lucia was herself exhibiting symptoms of schizophrenia during the years that he was at work on *Finnegans Wake,* although Joyce for a long time attempted to ignore the seriousness of her mental condition, and in Issy may have been working out in fiction the evidence of that condition, while writing a loving father's apologia for his child.

The most romantic prototype for Issy is the Iseult of medieval romance, and Chapelizod—the chapel of Izod/Iseult

("chempel of Isid" [*FW* 26.17])—provides the setting to
which old King Mark of Cornwall sent his nephew Tristram to
claim her for him. The cuckolded Mark serves as still another
lascivious old "geeser" in the *Wake,* and Tristram a variant of
the son who upends him:

Hohohoho, moulty Mark!
You're the rummest old rooster ever flopped out of a Noah's ark
And you think you're cock of the wark.
Fowls, up! Tristy's the spry young spark
That'll tread her and wed her and bed her and red her. (*FW* 383.8-12)

(That both Shem and Shaun see themselves in the enviable
role as the Tristram lover is apparent when Tristram-Tristan
evolves into "Treestone" (*FW* 113.19), combining the tree
emblem of Shem with the stone of Shaun.) Issy herself may see
the love triangle in which she plays her part reflected in
reverse in her mirror, where Mark of Cornwall becomes
"Kram of Llawnroc," and the nephew who plays the tactful
lover, Tristan is "Wehpen, luftcat revol, fairescapading in his
natsirt," while she herself is "Tuesy" (*FW* 388.2-4). Various
other rulers who lose their young brides to their entrusted
young emissaries provide parallels in the *Wake:* Finn MacCool,
Graine, and Diarmuid, and Arthur, Guinevere, and Lancelot.

No pattern in the *Wake* is ever complete without Joyce
being able to exact one more series of changes, ply a
corresponding motif through a seemingly discrete segment (as
the text asserts, "if you can spot fifty I spy four more" [*FW*
10.31]). If the narrative can provide "the tale of a Treestone
with one Ysold" (*FW* 113.19), how much more germane to
the presence of the two images of Issy (and the two maidens in
the park) if there were two Iseults, "twy Isas Boldmans" (*FW*
361.21). The variant treatments of the Tristram-Iseult story
allow for just such a pair, the Iseult of Ireland (known as Iseult
of the Fair Hair) whom he loves, and the Iseult of Brittany
(known as Iseult of the White Hands) whom he marries. In
Issy's monologue she conjures up the love situation in which
she is "isabeaubel" and her lover is "trysting of the tulipies"

(*FW* 146.17, 7), but also the man who "to be musband," as she nostalgically remembers, "I left on his shoulder one fair hair to guide hand" (*FW* 146.20, 25), assuming for herself the roles of both Iseults. And the possibility of two heroines opens the temptation for two heroes, two Tristrams for the contending personifiers, Shem and Shaun, each of whom sees himself as the great lover. In the person of Sir Amory Tristram, a member of Strongbow's invading force that reached Ireland in 1169, Joyce found the necessary corollary to Tristram of Lyonesse, one who also came by sea to Ireland under the direction of his monarch to establish a claim. Issy concludes her monologue with "Always, Amory, amor andmore" (*FW* 148.31), returning us to the opening section where "Sir Tristram, violer d'amores . . . had passencore rearrived from North Armorica" (*FW* 3.4-5).

The three junctures in *Finnegans Wake* where Issy appears most specifically are in the sixth, tenth, and fourteenth chapters: she addresses her mirror in coy, teasing, narcissistic tones, implying amorous liaisons that suggest the writing of a love letter; she assigns scurrilous footnotes to the children's night lessons, displaying a full range of sexual awareness, especially regarding the father's lustful intentions; and she responds to a love letter with a direct address that is both tender and passionate. Issy manifests sexual knowledge that subsumes that of the male participants: "He fell for my lips, for my lisp, for my lewd speaker. I felt for his strength, his manhood, his do you mind? There can be no candle to hold to it, can there?" (*FW* 459.28-30). And yet she is the picture of innocence, as the baby in the cot and the girl in the Mime, "IZOD . . . a bewitching blonde who dimples delightfully and is approached in loveliness only by her grateful sister reflection in a mirror" (*FW* 220.7-9). Duplicated throughout, Issy also expands into the seven colors of the rainbow, "Not Rose, Sevilla nor Citronelle; not Esmeralde, Pervinca nor Indra; not Viola even nor all of them four themes over" (*FW* 223.6-8). As these seven are the days of the week, so four times over they are the twenty-eight days of the month of February, with Issy herself as the twenty-ninth, the Leap Year Girl: "There's Ada, Bett, Celia, Delia, Ena, Fretta, Gilda, Hilda, Ita, Jess, Katty, Lou ... Mina, Nippa, Opsy, Poll, Queenie, Ruth, Saucy, Trix, Una, Vela, Wanda, Xenia, Yva, Zulma, Phoebe, Thelma. And Mee!" (*FW* 147.11-15). These appear in the Mime as "THE FLORAS (Girl Scouts from St. Bride's Finishing Establishment, demand acidulateds), a month's bunch of pretty maidens who, while they pick on her, their pet peeve, form with valkyrienne licence the guard for IZOD" (*FW* 220.3-7).

The relationship between Issy and Anna Livia is clearer than that between Earwicker and even his preferred son: she is an extension of her mother, even a "ghost" of the young Anna Livia. The woman in the *Wake* has a full existence, from infancy as the source of the Liffey river in Sally Gap to her maturity flowing through Dublin and her demise passing out into Dublin Bay. The closing section of the book records the death at dawn of the Liffey, "I'm passing out. O bitter ending! I'll slip away before they're up. They'll never see. Nor know. Nor miss me" (*FW* 627.34-36), to be drawn up as moisture into the clouds that will break as rain in the Wicklow Hills, reengendering the young river. Her life as a young girl is depicted in chapter 8, where two gossiping washerwomen, on either bank of the Liffey, reactivate old tales:

O
tell me all about
Anna Livia! I want to hear all
about Anna Livia. Well, you know Anna Livia? Yes, of course, we all know about Anna Livia. Tell me all. Tell me now. You'll die when you hear. (*FW* 196.1-6)

This washing of dirty linen in public recapitulates the adventure of a young Earwicker, a Scandinavian navigator, sailing up the river (between the legs of the young maiden) as a Viking invader, and settling down in Ireland, converting to Christianity and marrying Anna: "he was a heavy trudging lurching lieabroad of a Curraghman, making his hay for whose sun to shine on, as tough as the oaktrees (peats be with them!)

used to rustle that time down by the dykes of killing Kildare, for forstfellfoss with a plash across her. She thought she's sankh neathe the ground with nymphant shame when he gave her the tigris eye! O happy fault! Me wish it was he!" (*FW* 202.28-34).

The scandal that titivates the gossip concerns Earwicker's behavior in the park, and Anna Livia's presumed reaction to the ensuing rumors, but also her premarital escapades ("She must have been a gadaboumt in her day," speculates one of the washerwomen; "She had a flewmen of her owen," corroborates the other [*FW* 202.4-6]). Her affair in question involves her with a country priest:

Well, there once dwelt a local heremite, Michael Arklow was his riverend name ... and one venersderg in junojuly, oso sweet and so cool and so limber she looked, Nance the Nixie, Nanon L'Escaut, in the silence, of the sycamores, all listening, the kindling curves you simply can't stop feeling, he plunged both of his newly anointed hands, the core of his cushlas, in her singimari saffron strumans of hair, parting them and soothing her and mingling it, that was deepdark and ample like this red bog at sundown. By the Vale Vowclose's lucydlac, the reignbeau's heavenarches arronged orranged her. Afrothdizzying galbs, her enamelled eyes indergoading him on to the vierge violetian. (*FW* 203.17-29)

All of this is an old story, and both the teller and the listener know it well, but the excited narration nonetheless continues, as both gossips recreate in their dialogue the history of the river in which they sink their hands to wash the Earwickers' clothes. "If you don't like my story get out of the punt," the storyteller remarks with annoyance (*FW* 206.21), as Joyce's text calls attention to its own process, the twice-told tale reactivated on demand and in the constant flux of reanimation and revision.

The incident in Phoenix Park may have had its antecedent in Anna Livia's own girlish days when "she was licked by a hound, Chirripa-Chirruta, while poing her pee, pure and simple, on the spur of the hill in old Kippure" (*FW* 204.11-

13); thereafter she left the countryside and flowed into Dublin: "the wiggly livvly, she sideslipped out by a gap in the Devil's glen while Sally her nurse was sound asleep in a sloot and, feefee fiefie, fell over a spillway before she found her stride and lay and wriggled in all the stagnant black pools" (*FW* 204.14-18). When the rumor reaches full stride and circulates from pub to pub, flowing down the river from the neighbor's dirty drawers, the mature Anna Livia sets out to counteract their effect: "So she said to herself she'd frame a plan to fake a shine, the mischiefmaker" (*FW* 206.6-7). With determination Anna Livia "bergened a zakbag, a shammy mailsack, with the lend of a loan of the light of his lampion, off one of her swapsons, Shaun the Post" (*FW* 206.9-11), and after her ablutions, she proceeds to distribute various presents to all of her children: "with a Christmas box apiece for aisch and iveryone of her childer, the birthday gifts they dreamt they gabe her, the spoiled she fleetly laid at our door" (*FW* 209.27-29). (And Anna Livia Plurabelle has one hundred and eleven children [on a mythic scale] as the three ones line up to read 111.) In her guise as the legendary banshees of Ireland she gathers up the belongings of the slain ("And where in thunder did she plunder? Fore the battle or efter the ball?" [*FW* 209.12-13]), collecting and distributing being two facets of the same phenomenon. And as a pecking hen she collects the bits and pieces ("one of Biddy's beads went bobbing till she rounded up lost histereve" [*FW* 213.36-214.1]), including the mysterious letter of rumor and accusation that may have been thrown out onto the midden heap: "letters have never quite been their old selves since . . . to the shock of both, Biddy Doran looked at literature" (*FW* 112.24-27).

"Literature" in *Finnegans Wake* exists on the broadest margin imaginable, and beyond most margins imagined, and on a fundamental, interpersonal level includes all means of written correspondence—letters, telegrams, postcards, messages, advertisements, graffiti. A single letter of importance seems to dominate the concerns in the book, apparently paralleled by a contrasting, corrective letter (and numerous variants of these), just as the fate of the new Irish nation in 1923 wavered on the presumed existence of two treaties with the British government, known as Document Number One and Document Number Two: from "documans nonbar one" to "deckhuman amber too" (*FW* 358.30, 619.19). One assumes a letter accusing and a letter exonerating, the first mysteriously from an American cousin to a recipient in Ireland, from one Maggie to another, and the second written by Anna Livia in an effort to restore her husband's reputation, despite her own disgruntlement with him. Issy may well be the writer and the recipient of the scurrilous letter (in her role as the two Maggies), while Anna dictates the apologia, with Shem as her amanuensis, Shaun as letter carrier, and Earwicker himself as the nervous recipient, never quite sure which of the versions arrived in his morning post. The outer perimeter of communications offers the possibility that what arrives in the morning delivery is the daily newspaper, in which case Earwicker's indiscretion becomes communal knowledge. But letters can be censored or damaged or lost, intercepted and misinterpreted: a shortsighted reader while eating breakfast can jab a fork into the letter ("numerous stabs and foliated gashes made by a pronged instrument. These paper wounds, four in type, were gradually and correctly understood to mean stop, please stop, do please stop, and O do please stop respectively" [*FW* 124.2-5]), and a hen pecking at it in the kitchen midden can perform the same excisions: "the fourleaved shamrock or quadrifoil jab was more recurrent wherever the script was clear and the term terse and that these two were the selfsame spots naturally selected for her perforations by Dame Partlet on her dungheap" (*FW* 124.20-24).

A discarded letter, no longer wanted by its intended receiver, can turn up unexpectedly, but there are also implications that the "message" may not ever have been intended for a reader, that it is the private communication within which it somehow has its counterpart in a real letter outside. The dying Anna Livia fuses the two as she muses:

And watch would the letter you're wanting be coming may be. And cast ashore. That I prays for be mains of me draims. Scratching it and patching at with a prompt from a primer. And what scrips of nutsnolleges I pecked up me meself. Every letter is a hard but yours sure is the hardest crux ever. Hack an axe, hook an oxe, hath an an, heth hith ences. But once done, dealt and delivered, tattat, you're on the map. Rased on traumscrapt from Maston, Boss. After rounding his world of ancient days. Carried in a caddy or screwed and corked. On his mugisstosst surface. With a bob, bob, bottledby. Blob. When the waves give up yours the soil may for me. Sometime then, somewhere there, I wrote me hopes and buried the page. (*FW* 623.29-624.4)

The note awash in a bottle seems Earwicker's hopes of vindication, an exoneration that may be published in the *Boston Evening Transcript,* while the message of her hopes and dreams written by Anna Livia may be scratched up by the hen and exposed to the world. She secretly wants him to read the letter, from "the wisherwife, superscribed and subpencilled by yours A Laughable Party, with afterwrite, S.A.G., to Hyde and Cheek, Edenberry, Dubblenn, WC," wishes for its recovery ("till Cox's wife, twice Mrs Hahn, pokes her beak into the matter"), but worries that it will disappear forever: "will this kiribis pouch filled with litterish fragments lurk dormant in the paunch of that halpbrother of a herm, a pillarbox?" (*FW* 66.16-27).

Finnegans Wake poses the problem of a *Finnegans Wake* that never gets published, or if published is never read, or if read is lost in incomprehensibility, positing the condition by which any missive as small and easily overlooked as a letter, no matter how significant its matter, can disappear. Misdirected or misappropriated, "a loveletter, lostfully hers . . . would be lust on Ma" (*FW* 80.14-15). Time passes, people change, buildings are demolished, even civilizations disappear, and the letter proves undeliverable and is "rewritten" with a new message on its envelope, dooming it forever to the dead letter office: "No such parson. No such fender. No such lumber. No such race" (*FW* 63.11-12). Yet, regardless of its fortunes or its future, the epistle remains that which binds and involves all members of the family—in fact, everyone—all of whom play a part in its existence:

The elm that whimpers at the top told the stone that moans when stricken. Wind broke it. Wave bore it. Reed wrote it. Syce ran with it. Hand tore it and wild went war. Hen trieved it and plight pledged peace. It was folded with cunning, sealed with crime, uptied by a harlot, undone by a child. It was life but was it fair? It was free but was it art? The old hunks on the hill read it to perlection. It made ma make merry and sissy so shy and rubbed some shine off Shem and put some shame into Shaun. (*FW* 94.4-12)

The letter surfaces and resurfaces at various points in the *Wake,* in various segments and having undergone various changes. When first pecked up from the battlefield by a "peacefugle, a parody's bird," the salutation is missing and it begins in medias res with "But it's the armitides toonigh, militopucos, and toomourn we wish for a muddy kissmans to the minutia workers and there's to be a gorgeups truce for happinest childher everwere," and mentions "foder allmichael and a lugly parson of cates and howitzer muchears and midgers and maggets" (*FW* 11.9, 13-24). On one hand the letter celebrates peace on earth, and on the other it is a chatty communication asking about the members of the family. A later version seems a good deal more complete and somewhat clearer, and appears on a "goodishsized sheet of letterpaper originating by transhipt from Boston (Mass.)," with a date and salutation:

of the last of the first to Dear whom it proceded to mention Maggy well & allathome's health well only the hate turned the mild on *the van* Houtens and the general's elections with a *lovely* face of some born gentleman with a beautiful present of wedding cakes for dear thankyou Chriesty and with grand funferall of poor Father Michael don't forget unto life's & Muggy well how are you Maggy & hopes soon to hear well & must now close it with fondest to the twoinns with four crosskisses for holy paul holey corner holipoli wholyisland pee ess from (locust may eat all but this sign shall they never) affectionate largelooking tache of tch. (*FW* 111.8-20)

The signature is obliterated by a "stain, and that a teastain" (*FW* 111.20), which is in itself a signature: the letter comes from Boston, where a "teaparty" of "Indians" registered their displeasure with the King of England. The use of disguises parallels the hidden and elusive nature of language and of the letter itself.

During the children's night lessons Issy tries her hand at letter-writing, assisted in following prescribed modes by a maternal hand. Her effort recapitulates the familiar items of interest: "I and we (tender condolences for happy funeral, one if) so sorry to (mention person suppressed for the moment, F.M.). Well (enquiries after allhealths) how are you (question maggy). A lovely (introduce to domestic circles) pershan of cates" (*FW* 280.10-16). Although Earwicker may dread the letter that exposes his escapade in the park, the "Maggy" sort of epistle seems harmless enough, except perhaps for the *person suppressed for the moment,* whose initials are *F.M.* From *foder allmichael* to *poor Father Michael* the subject of the dead priest's funeral has wedged its way into the information transhipped in the letter, and an attempt to apply a measure of Marxist criticism (among many) to the letter had resulted in the conjecture "that Father Michael about this red time of the white terror equals the old regime and Margaret is the social revolution" (*FW* 116.7-8). For Anna Livia Plurabelle there had once been in the past (during *the old regime*) a premarital lover, "a local heremite, Michael Arklow was his riverend name" (*FW* 203.18-19), and it might well be this ancient affair that she would like to bury, to keep suppressed, while her daughter may maliciously seek to uncover it. Anna Livia's own letter, a fulsome one toward the closing of the book, buried the dead Father Michael even deeper. She prefers letters and newspapers that bring only the most innocuous news ("Pens picture at Manchem House Horsegardens shown in Morning post as from Boston transcripped"), and her recapitulations of the tidbits of the resurfacing letter will render them exclusively the subject of dreams, to be obliterated upon waking: "To hear that lovelade parson, of case, of a bawl

gentlemale, pour forther moracles. Don't forget! The grand
fooneral will now shortly occur. Remember. The remains
must be removed before eaght hours shorp. With earnestly
conceived hopes. So help us to witness to this day to hand in
sleep" (*FW* 617.22-29). The mother has no illusions that the
daughter is sexually precocious, acknowledging that Issy-
Maggy had "seen all" ("margarseen oil" [*FW* 615.31]).

As Anna Livia undertakes the letter that will exonerate her
guilty husband, she is actually focusing attention away from
her own past to concentrate on his. "Well, here's lettering you
erronymously anent other clerical fands allieged herewith,"
she asserts, dispelling without denying her complicity with the
cleric, but when it comes to "the Married Woman's Improperty
Act a correspondent paints out that the Swees Auburn vogue
is hanging down straith fitting to her innocenth eyes." The
perfidious woman that she would prefer to implicate is the
neighbor whose dirty drawers the washerwomen had
commented upon with titillation, the wife of the Cad who
encounters Earwicker in the park and opens up the subject of
his indiscretions, "The cad with the pope's wife, Lily Kinsella,
who became the wife of Mr Sneakers for her good name in the
hands of the kissing solicitor, will now engage in attentions"
(*FW* 617.30-618.6). As Biddy Doran she composes a succinct
account of Earwicker's sin:

Mesdaims, Marmouselles, Mescerfs! Silvapais! All schwants
(schwrites) ischt tell the cock's trootabout him. Kapak kapuk. No
minzies matter. He had to see life foully the plak and the smut,
(schwrites). There were three men in him (schwrites). Dancings
(schwrites) was his only ttoo feebles. With apple harlottes. And a
little mollvogels. Spissially (schwrites) when they peaches .... Add
dapple inn. (*FW* 113.11-18)

A closet full of skeletons rattle their bones throughout the
"events" of *Finnegans Wake,* yet always only within the realm
of possibilities, since all such events are presented as relayed
fictions. The epistolary clues are particularly incisive and

tantalizing, as when Napoleon dispatches to Arthur Wellesley, the Duke of Wellington ("Leaper Orthor. Fear siecken! Fieldgaze thy tiny frow. Hugacting. Nap" [*FW* 9.4-5]), or when Issy sends a postcard ("Dear old Erosmas. Very glad you are going to Penmark. Write to the corner. Grunny Grant" [*FW* 301.n5]), or Shem advertises in the personal column ("Jymes wishes to hear from wearers of abandoned female costumes . . . He has lately commited one of the then commandments but she will now assist. . . . He appreciates it. Copies. ABORTISEMENT" [*FW* 181.27-33]), or we read the writing on the wall ("Stand up, mickos! Make strake for minnas! By order, Nicholas Proud" [*FW* 12.24-25]) or the title of a book ("*How A Guy Finks and Fawkes When He Is Going Batty,* by Maistre Sheames de la Plume" [*FW* 177.29-30]). All forms of written comunication conspire to suggest the worst about all of the people involved, as do various forms of oral language: the *Wake* combines numerous methods of storytelling, written and spoken, and departs from the traditional printed fiction not in the peculiarities of its linguistic distortions as much as in the broken forms of narration, the balance between what the reader senses as *heard* and what is assumed to be *read,* despite the fact that all aspects of the text are being read. Just as Anna Livia offers scores of titles for her mamafesta, so Earwicker is barraged by almost as many insulting epithets shouted at him by a besieging antagonist. *Finnegans Wake* as a text aspires mostly to the dramatic form, which allows both a reading of a printed script and the speaking of the parts by actors.

"The Mime of Mick, Nick and the Maggies" presents one dramatic approximation of the interaction of the universal family, and is in itself an adaptation from a preceding text ("adopted from the Ballymooney Bloodriddon Murther by Bluechin Blackdillain" [*FW* 219.21]), while the actors playing the parts are themselves interchanged ("nightly redistribution of parts and players by the puppetry producer and daily dubbing of ghosters" [*FW* 219.7-8]). The basic family, most often identified as Humphrey Chimpden Earwicker, Anna

Livia Plurabelle, Shem, Shaun, and Issy, but in the mock-dawn
scene assumed to be Mr. and Mrs. Porter, Jerry, Kevin, and
Isobel, are here HUMP, ANN, GLUGG, CHUFF, and IZOD,
with KATE as the charwoman, SAUNDERSON as the pub
curate, THE FLORAS as the Girls from St. Brides's, and THE
CUSTOMERS as the twelve in the pub. Despite the designation
of "mime," the drama evolves in spoken language, and of
particular importance is the guessing of the magic word
"heliotrope." In the dawn episode, however, a sort of glaring
literalness of image dominates the "dumbshow," where each
item of furniture in the bedroom is presented as an
unambiguous stage direction: "Chamber scene. Boxed. Ordinary
bedroom set. Salmonpapered walls. Back, empty Irish grate. . . .
Over mantelpiece picture of Michael, lance, slaying Satan,
dragon with smoke," etc. (*FW* 559.1-16). Of unusual starkness
is the depiction of the aging husband and wife, where image is
effected by the use of the most explicit pictographic language:

Man looking round, beastly expression, fishy eyes, paralleliped
homoplatts, ghazometron pondus, exhibits rage, Business. Ruddy
blond, Armenian bole, black patch, beer wig, gross build, episcopalian,
any age. Woman, sitting, looks at ceiling, haggish expression, peaky
nose, trekant mouth, fithery wight, exhibits fear. Welshrabbit teint,
Nubian shine, nasal fossette, turfy tuft, undersized, free kirk, no age.
Closeup. Play! (*FW* 559.22-29)

The parents have been awakened by the cry of one of the
children (Jerry has wet his bed), but the time warp allows for a
view of the older parents, when the children are also grown, at
an instance when the children are in their cots. The tableau is
exceptionally vivid—"Man with nightcap, in bed, fore.
Woman, with curlpins, hind" (*FW* 559.20)—yet carefully hidden within language: the *beer wig,* for example, is not as much
a tangible article of attire as it is a designation for Earwicker,
whose name derives from the earwig which presumably causes
dreams by lodging in the sleeper's ear.

The "voices" of all five characters at times break through to
be heard, often in self-defense, sometimes in accusation, even

on occasion in discursive narration. Shem, whose medium is the written word, can be heard in disingenuous tones taunting Shaun about the writing of the letter: "could you, of course, decent Lettrechaun, we knew (to change your name of not your nation) while still in the barrel, read the strangewrote ana-glyptics of those shemletters patent for His Christian's Em?" (*FW* 419.15-18). Shaun, whose talents are for the "blarneyest blather in all Corneywall" (*FW* 419.15), is discernible in his various moods and tones, not least which is his righteous bluster: "HeCitEncy! Your words grates on my ares. Notorious I rather would feel inclined to myself in the first place to describe Mr O'Shem the Draper with before letter as should I be accentually called upon for a dieoguinnsis to pass my opinions, properly spewing, into impulsory irelitz" (*FW* 421.23-27). Issy, who writes the way she talks, responds to Shaun-Jaun's love speech by saying, "listen, Jaunick, accept this witwee's mite, though a jennyteeny witween piece torn in one place from my hands in second place of a linenhall valen-tino with my fondest and much left to tutor. . . . It was heavily bulledicted for young Fr Ml, my pettest parriage priest" (*FW* 457.36-458.4), but also appends footnotes that are implosively vocal: "Heavenly twinges, if it's one of his I'll fearly feint as swoon as he enterrooms" (*FW* 278.n4).

The most distinctive voice in the *Wake* is that of Anna Livia passing out to sea during the closing pages, although very little is ever heard of her voice during the course of the book. In the washerwomen sequence something akin to a prose poem is included, apparently a statement by Anna Livia, but shaped into the form of a more formal discourse than actual speech and introduced as "Anna Livia's cushingloo that was writ by one and rede by two and trouved by a poule in the parco." This "lullably" involves concerns quite appropriate for a river: *"By earth and the cloudy but I badly want a brandnew bankside, bedamp and I do, and a plumper at that!"* (*FW* 200.36-201.6). During the séance in which various spook voices discuss the Earwicker misdemeanor, Anna Livia's reply is recorded, but one suspects that as she denounces the two temptresses who misled her husband, and the "Sully" whom she accuses of spreading the lies about him, the nature of her discourse approaches the formal writing of a counterbrief, a letter in defense. "I will confess to his sins and blush me further," she says in what sounds like speech, but "Responsif you plais" introduces letter-writing conventions, and the tirade against Sully, "a barracker associated with tinkers, the blackhand, Shovellyvans," terms him a "wreuter of annoyimgmost letters and skirriless ballets in Parsee Franch." Yet her tone is extremely conversational ("He cawls me Granny-stream-Auborne when I am hiding under my hair from him and I cool him my Finnyking he's so joyant a bounder"), until we notice the use of the Honi Soit variant found in a previous letter, and the final signature: "Respect. S.V.P. Your wife. Amn. Anm. Amm. Ann" (*FW* 494.30,495.33).

It is as tempting to identify Anna Livia with the washerwomen on her banks as it is to consider Biddy the hen her avatar, especially when Shem invokes her as "our turf-brown mummy . . . running with her tidings . . . all her rillringlets shaking . . . little oldfashioned mummy, little wonderful mummy, ducking under bridges . . . slipping sly by Sallynoggin, as happy as the day is wet, babbling, bubbling, chattering to herself, deloothering the fields on their elbows, leaning with the sloothering slide of her, giddygaddy, grannyma, gossipaceous Anna Livia" (*FW* 194.22-195.4). The bansheelike washerwomen can be heard once again as the final chapter moves toward Anna Livia's last letter and her last soliloquy: "Caffirs and culls and onceagain overalls, the fittest surviva lives that blued, iorn and storridge can make them" (*FW* 614.10-12). The laundry has come back from "Annone Wishwashwhose . . . blanches bountifully" (*FW* 614.2-4), but Anna Livia's letter stirs up the dirt once again as she denounces the raking up of muck against Earwicker: "Mucksrats which bring up about uhrweckers they will come to know good" (*FW* 615.16-17). The park events are dismissed as nothing more than a bad dream ("When he woke up in a sweat besidus it was to pardon him" [*FW* 615.22-23]), and her long epistle concludes with her version of a newly awakened, newly reborn Earwicker: "The herewaker of our hamefame is his real namesame who will get himself up and erect, confident and heroic when but, young as of old, for my daily comfreshenall, a wee one woos"—to which she signs herself quite unequivocally, "Alma Luvia, Pollabella" (*FW* 619.11-16). But the postscript implies that there is also another letter, *deckhuman amber too,* which belongs to "Soldier Rollo's sweetheart" (*FW* 619.17)—apparently Issy.

Nothing quite prepares us for the speaking voice of Anna Livia Plurabelle. Her soliloquy is as the river addressing her husband, the city: "Soft morning, city! Lsp! I am leafy speafing. Lpf" (*FW* 619.20). It is dawn as it is early autumn, and she seeks to rouse the husband from his sleep so that they might stroll about before the children are awake, to recapture the memories of their young days together. Anna Liffey is once again her young self, and the soliloquy carries her from youth in the countryside through maturity in Dublin, and old age and death in Dublin Bay. Most of her speech concerns the young days, in sweetness and innocence and gentle nostalgia. She comments patiently about the contrary twins and the daughter that her husband had so much wanted to have, but prefers to let them sleep while the two of them revisit old haunts and recall pleasant memories. She tends to blame the washerwomen for the differences between her sons ("Maybe it's those two old crony aunts held them out to the water front. Queer Mrs Quickenough and odd Miss Doddpebble. And when them two has had a good few there isn't much more dirty clothes to publish" [*FW* 620.18-21]), but with no particular tone of recrimination. The world for Anna Livia has been washed clean in the morning and she has few harsh words for anyone, or unkindnesses to remember, even to assuming the personae of the two temptresses as mistaken aspects of herself: "Our native night when you twicetook me for some Marienne Sherry and then your Jermyn cousin who signs hers with exes" (*FW* 624.36-625.2). Instead she concentrates on the wooing that won her, as she reaffirms her marriage vows: "you

were the pantymammy's Vulking Corsergoth. The invision of
Indelond. And, by Thorror, you looked it! My lips went livid
for from the joy of fear. Like almost now. How? How you said
how you'd give me the keys of me heart. And we'd be married
till delth to uspart. And though dev do espart" (*FW*
626.27-32).

A subtle change, however, eventually begins to take place: as
the fresh water from the hills passes under Island Bridge at the
edge of Dublin, it meets the brackish water from the sea ("Sea,
sea! Here, weir, reach island, bridge" [*FW* 626.7]). The Liffey
through the centuries has had its difficulties, freezing over,
drying up, flooding; and Anna remembers her personal troubles, although she manages to take them in stride. Instead, she
looks ahead to her demise, and a note of remorse and even
bitterness creeps into her voice as she accepts the inevitable
but is nonetheless resentful, seeing herself replaced in her
husband's affections by her daughter: "Yes, you're changing,
sonhusband, and you're turning, I can feel you, for a
daughterwife from the hills again. Imlamaya. And she is
coming. Swimming in my hindmoist. Diveltaking on me tail.
Just a whisk brisk sly spry spink spank sprint of a thing
theresomere, saultering. Saltarella come to her own" (*FW*
627.1-6). Her inclinations now are to remain philosophic
about the change, but also to reaffirm in strong terms her own
worth, her superiority and that of her ancestry, demeaning the
commonness and insignificance of the *Vulking Corsergoth* as
a mere and fallible mortal:

How small it's all! And me letting on to meself always. And lilting on
all the time. I thought you were all glittering with the noblest of
carriage. You're only a bumpkin. I thought you the great in all things,
in guilt and in glory. You're but a puny. Home! My people were not
their sort out beyond there so far as I can. . . . But I'm loothing them
that's here and all I lothe. Loonely in me loneness. For all their faults.
(*FW* 627.20-34)

And with just a moment of fear at the tremulous end, Anna
Livia passes out to sea; the leaves that she had carried along are
all gone, except for the last leaf of winter.

Earwicker's voice is unmistakable when his characteristic stutter impedes his speech, the stutter serving orally as the mark of guilt to parallel the written word that incriminated Richard Pigott (hesitency) and proved that the letter from Parnell approving of the Phoenix Park murders was a forgery ("HeCitEncy" contains Earwicker's initials [*FW* 421.23]). In the same park Earwicker has encountered the two girls and three soldiers, and in the park soon after he encounters the Cad with a pipe who asks him the time. His guilty reaction is immediate, as he swears on the Bible (and the Wellington Monument mistaken as a crucifix) that he is British, Anglican, and a businessman: "for the honours of our mewmew mutual daughters, credit me, I am woowoo willing to take my stand, sir, upon the monument, that sign of our ruru redemption . . . that there is not one tittle of truth, allow me to tell you, in that purest of fibfib fabrications" (*FW* 36.22-34). In this first scene of confrontation no single element of the incident itself is ever mentioned by either party, although Earwicker's reference to "daughters" should appear suspect. From the encounter the rumors spread nonetheless, so that when Earwicker's voice is heard on the radio ("Mass Taverner's at the mike again!"), the vague insistence of innocence merely duplicates the initial statement: "Meggeg, m'gay chapjappy fellow, I call our univalse to witness, as sicker as moyliffey eggs is known by our good househalters from yorehunderts of mamooth to be which they commercially are in ahoy high British quarters (conventional!) my guesthouse and cowhaendel credits will immediately stand ohoh open as straight as that neighbouring monument's fabrication . . . before the Great Schoolmaster's. (I tell you no story)" (*FW* 54.21-55.2). And indeed, no story gets told, except by rumor and innuendo, and it is not until Earwicker is confronted at the beerpull of his pub by the customers that he is forced into a far more elaborate explanation of events.

"Guilty but fellows culpows!" he declares (*FW* 363.20), and although he admits that "for every dime he yawpens that momouth you could park your ford in it" (*FW* 364.15-16), there is very little of the familiar stammer in this long self-defense. Although he begins with some degree of stumbling speech in his denunciation of those who accused him ("It was felt by me sindeade, that submerged doughdoughty doubleface told waterside labourers" (*FW* 363.20-21), and ends with a denunciation of the Brutus-Cassius duo that seeks to assassinate him ("when booboob brutals and cautiouses only aims at the oggog hogs in the humand" [*FW* 366.25-26]), Earwicker holds his own well in his defense, perhaps because he has dropped the pretense of total innocence and given up the ruse of pretending to be a loyal British subject and solid bourgeois. Admitting guilt—but with extenuating circumstances (the Happy Fault of St. Augustine's *O felix culpa*), he confronts the issues to a certain extent, at least acknowledging the nature of the accusation: "that I am the catasthmatic old ruffin sippahsedly improctor to be seducint trovatellas, the dire daffy damedeaconesses"—which he dismisses as "Fall stuff" (*FW* 366.22-30). The implication is that the situation with the two girls derives from a production of *A Royal Divorce,* which concerns Napoleon and his two wives (W.W. Kelly having starred as the Emperor): "My little love apprencisses, my dears, the estelles, van Nessies von Nixies voon der pool, which I had a reyal devouts for yet was it marly lowease or just a feel with these which olderman K. K. Alwayswelly he is showing ot the full nights" (*FW* 365.27-31). He admits to having urinated and defecated in the park after the theater, when no public convenience was open, but denies adulterous fornication: "selled my how hot peas after theactrisscalls from my imprecurious position and though achance I could have emptied a pan of backslop down drain by while of dodging a rere from the middenprivet appurtenant thereof, salving the presents of the board of wumps and pumps, I am ever incapable, where release of prisonals properly is concerned, of unlifting upfallen girls wherein dangered from them in thereopen out of unadulteratous bowery, with those hintering influences from an angelsexonism" (*FW* 363.27-35).

In his apologia Earwicker reveals a knowledge of the contents of the letter from Boston, beginning with "Dear and lest
I forget mergers and bow to you low, marchers!" (*FW* 364.11-
12)—"and well shoving off a boastonmess like lots wives does
over her handpicked hunsbend, as she would be calling, well,
for further oil mircles upon all herwayferer gods and rea-
nouncing my deviltries as was I a locally person of caves until I
got my purchase on her firmforhold I am, I like to think, by
their sacreligion of daimond cap daimond, confessedly in my
baron gentilhomme to the manhor bourne" (*FW* 364.35-
365.5). If these particular elements from the letter in any way
disconcert him he does not show it, nor does the name of
Father Michael indicate an awareness on his part of an element from his wife's past. It should have been apparent from
the early reference by Earwicker to "athome's health" (*FW*
363.22) that he was familiar with the contents of the letter and
that they held no apparent worries for him, even at this
instance when, with his back against the wall and facing the
heckling customers, he is at his most vulnerable. The letter is
after all a family affair ("Letter, carried of Shuan, son of Hek,
written of Shem, brother of Shaun, uttered for Alp, mother of
Shem, for Hek, father of Shaun" [*FW* 420.17-19]), and cycles
about among its members, the property of writer and reader,
finder and deliverer. And particularly revealing in Earwicker's
account is his awareness that he has been dreaming about his
own daughter: "I reveal thus my deepseep daughter which was
bourne up pridely out of medsdreams unclouthed when I was
pillowing in my brime" (*FW* 366.13-15).

Yet nothing much remains on an even keel for long in
Finnegans Wake, so when Earwicker's voice is next heard,
responding during the séance, the blustering denials and avo-
wals of innocence return, along with the guilty stammer:

On my verawife I never was nor can afford to be guilty of crim crig
con of malfeasance trespass against parson with the person of a
youthful gigirl frifrif friend chirped Apples, acted by Miss Dashe, and
with Any of my cousines in Kissilov's Slutsgartern or Gigglotte's Hill,

when I would touch to her dot and feel most greenily of her unripe
ones as it should prove most anniece and far too bahad, nieceless to
say, to my reputation on Babbyl Malket for daughters-in-trade being
lightly clad. (*FW* 532.18-26)

This stuttering defensiveness does not last long, however.
Cheered on by the Four Old Men (Mamalujo—*Ma*tthew,
*Ma*rk, *Lu*ke, and *Jo*hn), Earwicker delivers an extensive monologue in his guise as the city of Dublin. As such he boasts of his
civic achievements, from the founding of the town by the
Vikings to its development by the English, through every
stage of city-building and laying out of streets and raising of
towers and building of bridges over the Liffey. He recapitulates
the tale told by the washerwomen of the Viking conqueror of
Anna Liffey ("I upreized my magicianer's puntpole, the tri-
dont sired a tritan stock . . . and I abridged with domfine
norsemanship till I had done abate her maidan race, my
baresark bridge, and knew her fleshly when with all my bawdy
did I her whorship, min bryllupswibe" (*FW* 547.23-28).
Although shot through with urban blight and tenements and
overcrowding, the city rises to the skies, its glitter and glory in
honor of the river-bride. In relation to such grandeur and
accomplishment the incident in the park pales into insignificance, evolves into the figures on the Dublin coat of
arms: "These be my genteelician arms," Earwicker announces;
"At the crest, two young frish, etoiled, flappant, devoiled of
their habiliments, vested sable, withdrewers argent. For the
boss a coleopter, pondant, partifesswise, blazoned sinister, at
the slough, proper. In the lower field a terce of lanciers,
shaking unsheathed shafts, their arms crossed in saltire,
embusked, sinople" (*FW* 546.5-10).

All exigencies in the *Wake* remain operative: Earwicker
guilty or innocent, executed or exonerated; the crime a misdemeanor or felony, the sin venial or mortal. The "municipal sin
business" that occurred on "that tragoady thundersday" (*FW*
5.13-14) is at once a civic disorder, a moral offense, a commercial manipulation, a tragedy—and yet only as a staged piece of
dramatic literature, a story enacted—or only a rumor of scan-

dal, a bruiting about of a bit of gossip, a "hubbub caused in Edenborough" (*FW* 29.35-36). Nor is there any real evidence that anything actually has happened (or will happen), or that there is any actual narrative possible from the disjointed clues spread throughout the text. Instead of narrative events *Finnegans Wake* may essentially be a network of thematic structures held together by narrative bits from preexisting texts, the cultural flotsam and jetsam of human civilization, its literary and oral storytelling traditions. The fall of Earwicker parallels the fall of Adam from grace in the Garden of Eden, that initial Phoenix Park, the crucifixion of Christ at Calvary, the defeat of Napoleon at Waterloo, and (not to exclude a Lewis Carroll text) the fall of Humpty Dumpty from the wall. At ground level the motif involves an Irish-American ballad of the hodcarrier Tim Finnegan, whose fall from a ladder and subsequent death occasions a wake at which a bottle of whiskey hurled during a fracas smashes over the dead man, the spilled whiskey bringing him back to life. To complement the mundane Finnegan there is the Irish hero Finn MacCool, the buried giant whose resurrection is expected to signal the revival of the Irish nation: "Hohohoho, Mister Finn, you're going to be Mister Finnagain!" (*FW* 5.9-10).

At the level of H. C. Earwicker the intimation of a fall in reputation can excite a tempest in a teapot, although his wife in the morning calls upon him to awake from his guilty dream, "Rise up, man of the hooths, you have slept so long!" (*FW* 619.25-26), and encourages him to a restoration of his dignity: "And stand up tall! Straight. I want to see you looking fine for me" (*FW* 620.1-2). In her bitterer moments, however, she derides him as a bumpkin and a puny. Nonetheless, as the story is told and retold ("Jehu will tell to Christianer, saint to sage"), the incidents are augmented to epic proportions, "the humphriad of that fall and rise" (*FW* 53.8-9), so that they constantly move toward and away from a narrative focus. Just as Chapelizod exists as a prosaic Dublin suburb (where Mr. Duffy of "A Painful Case" resided) as well as the chapel of the legendary Iseult, so Phoenix Park has its gradations of significance: it owes its name to a linguistic misapprehension, the Irish *fionn-uisge* (white water) mistaken by the English as Phoenix, and a statue of the bird of resurrection placed in the park. Falling in flames to its death, the mythical Phoenix rises reborn from its ashes. Past, present, and future coexist in the *Wake,* the living tree petrifies into stone: "But was iz! Iseut? Ere were sewers! The oaks of ald now they lie in peat yet elms leap where askes lay. Phall if you but will, rise you must: and none so soon either shall the pharse for the nunce come down to a setdown secular phoenish" (*FW* 4.14-17).

As monumental and complex as *Finnegans Wake* is for any reader, its narrative elements can on close examination reduce themselves to minute proportions. The book that Shem is constructing unfolds "all marryvoising moodmoulded cyclewheeling history," yet reflects "from his own individual person life unlivable, transaccidentated through the slow fires of consciousness into a dividual chaos, perilous, potent, common to allflesh, human only, mortal" (*FW* 186.1-6)—himself alone, himself in conflict with himself, from all-powerful to merely human. Shem in opposition to Shaun represents all conflict; fused into the person of the father they interlock into a unity but break apart and polarize. Husband and wife merge as one, but divide all of male and female nature between them, and mother and daughter divide generations between them. In the *Wake* all of human history can be read as the story of a family of five, developed from a balance of two—male and female principles. As named personages they assume identities, but names and identities change, and it becomes possible that even nomenclature and language itself are already expanded versions of things far more basic. Pictographs, idiograms, hieroglyphics, claybooks, steles, runes: the implication of prehistoric signs that anticipate language may well stand for the principals themselves:

> the initials majuscule of Earwicker: the meant to be baffling chrismon trilithon sign ᗰ, finally called after some his hes hecitency Hec, which, moved contrawatchwise, represents his title

in sigla as the smaller Δ, fontly called following a certain change of state of grace of nature alp or delta, when single, stands for or tautologically stands beside the consort. (*FW* 119.16-22)

The florid and prestigious names of Humphrey Chimpden Earwicker and Anna Livia Plurabelle are far more often telescoped into their initials, H. C. E. and A. L. P., and even more often reduced to anagrammatic variations and initials imbedded in other words, the figure of the buried giant in the landscape, the flow of the river through the countryside and the city, the omnipresence of the cityscape itself. At a more microscopic level—at the level of runes—the letter E, turned face down or face up or facing itself, stands for the hero, as the deltic triangle stands for the heroine, and as a family and an enterprise (the pub, its help, and customers), and as the book of *Finnegans Wake* itself, everything can be collapsed into a footnote that is as concise as it is all-inclusive:

The Doodles family, ᗰ Δ ⊣ ✕ □ ∧ ⊏.
Hoodle doodle, fam.? (*FW* 299.n4)

7

In Lieu of an Ending

Whatever plans James Joyce may have had for a work to follow *Finnegans Wake* remain a mystery, although some rumors were available: he is presumed to have commented that his next book would be a simple one, and also that, having written a book about a river in the *Wake,* his next project would be a book about the sea. Not as frequently quoted is a comment that he made to a Zurich friend, that in admiration of the Greek resistance to the invasion of Fascist Italy he was contemplating writing a Greek tragedy. In the year-and-a-half interval between the publication of the *Wake* and his death Joyce was a war refugee on the move, worried about hospitalization for his daughter and a neutral nation that would take him and his family, and may also have assumed that he was terminally ill—a fear that he could not voice lest Switzerland refuse entry to a moribund refugee. Joyce may well have been aware that *Finnegans Wake* would have no successor.

As *A Portrait* had established his reputation among a small circle of intellectuals, *Ulysses* brought international fame and notoriety, a combination that proved effective in placing James Joyce in the primary role as the major modernist writer of his age, and in the four decades since his death that reputation has strengthened considerably. The first half of the twentieth century produced such modernist masters as Virginia Woolf, Gertrude Stein, Marcel Proust, Thomas Mann, T. S. Eliot, Ezra Pound, Franz Kafka, Federico García Lorca, Wallace Stevens, and William Faulkner, yet the period should remain primarily recognizable as the Age of Joyce, just as in art it is the Age of Picasso. On one level *A Portrait of the Artist as a Young Man* continues to outsell all other novels in paperback—a commercial and popular success unexpected for so "difficult" a writer—while on another level *Ulysses* is probably the most written-about text in the academic world, certainly in America. And *Finnegans Wake* finds its way onto many a bookshelf, even if copies of it look too clean ever to have been read.

Joyce's worries that the Second World War would doom the sales for *Finnegans Wake* were well founded, and the plans that he had for a volume of four long essays to make the *Wake* more accessible were rendered inoperative. In 1941 Joseph Campbell and Henry Morton Robinson attempted to find a publisher for their *Skeleton Key to Finnegans Wake,* but to no avail, considering the lack of interest in the *Wake;* but a controversy that was almost a scandal as well regarding Thornton Wilder's *The Skin of Our Teeth* oddly enough created enough of a backlash interest to persuade the American publisher of *Finnegans Wake* to publish the *Skeleton Key* in 1944. Joyce studies never faltered from that moment on, especially in the United States, and to date there are over a hundred books on Joyce and well over a thousand articles in various scholarly journals. Several periodicals devoted exclusively to James Joyce have appeared over the past three decades; the two most successful are *A Wake Newslitter,* which began in 1961 and has only recently changed its format to a series of "Occasional Papers," and the *James Joyce Quarterly,* which has been consistently publishing since 1963. Something close to a definitive biography of Joyce was published in 1959 by Richard Ellmann and revised for the Joyce centenary year in 1982, and remains the single most valuable book for the reader of Joyce's works. The constant increase in scholarly and critical investigations of every one of Joyce's texts, but especially *Ulysses,* makes any attempt to offer a complete bibliography of secondary material impossible, and the student of Joyce should be directed first to *A Bibliography of James Joyce Studies* by Robert Deming, a revised edition of which was published in 1977, and to the "Current JJ Checklist" by Alan M. Cohn that runs consistently in the *James Joyce Quarterly.*

A Select Bibliography of Book-Length Studies

Beckett, Samuel, et al. *Our Exagmination Round His Factification for Incamination of Work in Progress*, 1929.

Gilbert, Stuart. *James Joyce's Ulysses*, 1930.

Budgen, Frank. *James Joyce and the Making of Ulysses*, 1934 (revised 1972).

Levin, Harry. *James Joyce*, 1941 (revised 1960).

Campbell, Joseph, and Henry Morton Robinson. *A Skeleton Key to Finnegans Wake*, 1944.

Kain, Richard M. *Fabulous Voyager: James Joyce's Ulysses*, 1947.

Givens, Seon, ed. *James Joyce: Two Decades of Criticism*, 1948 (revised 1963).

Tindall, William York. *James Joyce: His Way of Interpreting the Modern World*, 1950.

Kenner, Hugh. *Dublin's Joyce*, 1955.

Magalaner, Marvin, and Richard M. Kain. *Joyce: The Man, the Work, the Reputation*, 1956.

Noon, William T., SJ. *Joyce and Aquinas*, 1957.

Schutte, William. *Joyce and Shakespeare*, 1957.

Ellmann, Richard. *James Joyce*, 1959 (revised 1982).

Atherton, James S. *The Books at the Wake*, 1959 (revised 1974).

Tindall, William York. *A Reader's Guide to James Joyce*, 1959.

Magalaner, Marvin. *Time of Apprenticeship*, 1959.

Hodgart, Matthew J. C., and Mabel P. Worthington. *Song in the Works of James Joyce*, 1959.

Litz, A. Walton. *The Art of James Joyce*, 1961.

Goldberg, S. L. *The Classical Temper*, 1961.

Hart, Clive. *Structure and Motif in Finnegans Wake*, 1962.

Adams, Robert M. *Surface and Symbol: The Consistency of James Joyce's Ulysses*, 1962.

Hart, Clive. *A Concordance to Finnegans Wake*, 1963.

Hayman, David. *A First-Draft Version of Finnegans Wake*, 1963.

Prescott, Joseph. *Exploring James Joyce,* 1964.

Sultan, Stanley. *The Argument of Ulysses,* 1964.

Bonheim, Helmut. *Joyce's Benefictions,* 1964.

Benstock, Bernard. *Joyce-again's Wake,* 1965.

Dalton, Jack, and Clive Hart, eds. *Twelve and a Tilly,* 1965.

Scholes, Robert, and Richard M. Kain. *The Workshop of Daedalus,* 1965.

Burgess, Anthony. *ReJoyce* (also titled *Here Comes Everybody*), 1965.

Goldman, Arnold. *The Joyce Paradox,* 1966.

Blamires, Harry. *The Bloomsday Book,* 1966.

Staley, Thomas F., ed. *James Joyce Today,* 1966.

Adams, Robert M. *James Joyce: Common Sense and Beyond,* 1966.

Cixous, Hélène. *L'Exil de James Joyce,* 1968 (trans. *The Exile of James Joyce,* 1972).

O'Brien, Darcy. *The Conscience of James Joyce,* 1968.

Hart, Clive. *James Joyce's Ulysses,* 1968.

Thornton, Weldon. *Allusions in Ulysses,* 1968.

Solomon, Margaret. *Eternal Geomater,* 1969.

Beck, Warren. *Joyce's Dubliners: Substance, Vision, and Art,* 1969.

Hart, Clive, ed. *James Joyce's Dubliners: Critical Essays,* 1969.

Tindall, William York. *A Reader's Guide to Finnegans Wake,* 1969.

Hayman, David. *Ulysses: The Mechanics of Meaning,* 1970 (revised 1982).

Staley, Thomas F., and Bernard Benstock, eds. *Approaches to Ulysses,* 1970.

Epstein, Edmund. *The Ordeal of Stephen Dedalus,* 1971.

Brandabur, Edward. *A Scrupulous Meanness: A Study of Joyce's Early Work,* 1971.

Ellmann, Richard. *Ulysses on the Liffey,* 1972.

Senn, Fritz, ed. *New Light on Joyce from the Dublin Symposium,* 1972.

Shechner, Mark. *Joyce in Nighttown,* 1974.

Gifford, Don, with Robert J. Seidman. *Notes for Joyce,* 1974.

Hart, Clive, and David Hayman, eds. *James Joyce's Ulysses: Critical Essays,* 1974.

Staley, Thomas F., ed. *Ulysses: Fifty Years,* 1974.

Bowen, Zack. *Musical Allusions in the Works of James Joyce,* 1974.

Hart, Clive, and Leo Knuth. *A Topographical Guide to James Joyce's Ulysses,* 1975.

Begnal, Michael, and Grace Eckley. *Narrator and Character in Finnegans Wake*, 1975.

Norris, Margot. *The Decentered Universe of Finnegans Wake*, 1976.

French, Marilyn. *The Book as World*, 1976.

Seidel, Michael. *Epic Geography*, 1976.

Begnal, Michael, and Fritz Senn. *A Conceptual Guide to Finnegans Wake*, 1976.

McHugh, Roland. *The Sigla of Finnegans Wake*, 1976.

Glasheen, Adaline. *A Third Census of Finnegans Wake*, 1977.

Ellmann, Richard. *The Consciousness of James Joyce*, 1977.

Peake, Charles H. *James Joyce: The Citizen and the Artist*, 1977.

Benstock, Bernard. *James Joyce: The Undiscover'd Country*, 1977.

Groden, Michael. *Ulysses in Progress*, 1977.

Raleigh, John Henry. *The Chronicle of Leopold and Molly Bloom*, 1977.

Staley, Thomas F., and Bernard Benstock, eds. *Approaches to Joyce's Portrait*, 1977.

Mink, Louis O. *A Finnegans Wake Gazetteer*, 1978.

Henke, Suzette A. *Joyce's Moraculous Sindbook*, 1978.

MacCabe, Colin. *James Joyce and the Revolution of the Word*, 1978.

Maddox, James. *James Joyce and the Assault upon Character*, 1978.

Kenner, Hugh. *Joyce's Voices*, 1978.

Boyle, Robert R., SJ. *James Joyce's Pauline Vision*, 1978.

DiBernard, Barbara. *Alchemy in Finnegans Wake*, 1980.

Gose, Elliott B., Jr. *The Transformation Process in Joyce's Ulysses*, 1980.

Brivic, Sheldon. *Joyce between Freud and Jung*, 1980.

Gottfried, Roy K. *The Art of Joyce's Syntax in Ulysses*, 1980.

McCarthy, Patrick. *The Riddles of Finnegans Wake*, 1980.

Kenner, Hugh. *Ulysses*, 1980.

Benstock, Shari, and Bernard Benstock. *Who's He When He's at Home: A James Joyce Directory*, 1980.

Manganiello, Dominic. *Joyce's Politics*, 1980.

McHugh, Roland. *Annotations to Finnegans Wake*, 1980.

Reynolds, Mary. *Joyce and Dante*, 1981.

Cope, Jackson I. *Joyce's Cities*, 1981.

Lawrence, Karen. *The Odyssey of Style in Ulysses*, 1981.

Epstein, E. L., ed. *A Starchamber Quiry*, 1982.

Thomas, Brook. *James Joyce's Ulysses: A Book of Many Happy Returns*, 1982.

Benstock, Bernard, ed. *The Seventh of Joyce*, 1982.

Gifford, Don. *Joyce Annotated*, 1982.

Bushrui, S. B., and Bernard Benstock, eds. *James Joyce: An International Perspective*, 1982.

Henke, Suzette A., and Elaine Unkeless, eds. *Women in Joyce*, 1982.

MacCabe, Colin, ed. *James Joyce: New Perspectives*, 1982.

McCormack, W. J., and Alistair Stead, eds. *James Joyce and Modern Literature*, 1982.

Riquelme, John Paul. *Teller and Tale in Joyce's Fiction*, 1983.

Peterson, Richard F., Alan M. Cohn, and Edmund L. Epstein, eds. *Work in Progress: Joyce Centenary Essays*, 1983.

Rose, Danis, and John O'Hanlon. *Understanding Finnegans Wake*, 1983.

Scott, Bonnie K. *Joyce and Feminism*, 1984.

Benstock, Bernard, ed. *Critical Essays on James Joyce*, 1984.

Index